The Woman's Dress for Success Book

The Woman's DRESS FOR SUCCESS Book

John T. Molloy

WARNER BOOKS

A Time Warner Company

WARNER BOOKS EDITION

Library of Congress Catalog Card Number 77-81320
ISBN 0-446-38586-7 (U.S.A.)

This Warner Books Edition is published by arrangement with Follett Publishing Company.

Warner Books, Inc., 1271 Avenue of the Americas, New York, NY 10020

Printed in the United States of America

First Printing: September 1978

30 29 28 27 26 25

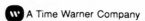 A Time Warner Company

To my wife and best friend, Maureen.

Contents

Acknowledgments

I would like to express my special thanks to my editor, Pat Reardon. His patience and professional skill made this book possible.

I owe thanks to my client corporations who supplied the money for much of the research reported on in this book, particularly to one large company with a large heart which allowed me to use specific information that it owned.

I would also like to thank the thousands of men and women who filled out forms and answered my research questions.

JOHN T. MOLLOY

The Woman's Dress for
Success Book

Introduction

The Mistakes Women Make and How to Correct Them

This is the most important book ever written about women's clothes because it is based on scientific research, not on opinion.

The advice in this book will help women make substantial gains in business and in their social lives. It should also revolutionize their clothes-buying habits.

Most American women dress for *failure*. I have said that before about men, and research shows that it applies equally to women. Women dress for failure because they make three mistakes.

1. They let the fashion industry influence their choice of business clothes.
2. They often still view themselves mainly as sex objects.
3. They let their socioeconomic background influence their choice of clothing.

The only reasonable alternative is for women to let science help them choose their clothes.

The name of the science I practice is wardrobe engineering. The idea is to use research data to manipulate the dress of an individual to draw a favorable response from the people he or she meets. This is done by testing how various groups react to standard modes of dress.

That sounds simple, but it is an elaborate process that involves sophisticated data-collecting techniques. After the information is collected, it is analyzed and stored in computers. We now have a multimillion-dollar bank of information.

The results of wardrobe engineering can be remarkable. By making adjustments in a woman's wardrobe, we can make her look more successful and better educated. We can increase her chances of success in the business world; we can increase her chances of becoming a top executive; and we can make her more attractive to various types of men.

Notice that I said "can," and not "will." What wardrobe engineering *will* do is give women a better statistical edge in all of those areas.

The term *manipulate* may strike you as sinister. It's not. Wardrobe engineering, like all sciences, is really amoral. In our money-oriented, status-conscious society, most people want to succeed. And you stand a much better chance of succeeding if you know what research has determined to be the look of success.

Two stories illustrate how wardrobe adjustments can point women toward success.

An accounting firm called me in to work with a promising young woman who was having trouble.

Executives of the firm outlined the problem: The woman had all the academic credentials and was a star tax consultant when she worked at the home office. But when she went to client companies' offices to work on their books and advise officials, the executives invariably ignored her sound advice.

When I met her, the problem was obvious. She was four feet eleven inches, ninety-two pounds, blonde, and "cute." She was twenty-six and looked sixteen.

I decked her out in every authority symbol her tiny frame could hold—dark suits with contrasting white blouses, silk scarves, brimmed hats. She even went several steps further, including wearing glasses with heavy black frames.

Severity carried the day. Clients listened so well that she now is one of the few women partners in the firm.

Not every businesswoman need transform herself from fawn to barracuda, as the following story shows: The woman, a sales engineer, was five feet eight inches and big-boned. She started her career in the Northeast but was transferred. After her transfer she was approaching customers in South Carolina, wearing dark suits and lugging an imposing, masculine-looking attaché case. Not many were buying.

I put her in light-colored suits and dresses and traded in her bulky attaché case for a more feminine version. She went soft, Southern, and successful—better than 25 percent more successful, in fact.

WHY FASHION FAILS YOU

Letting the fashion industry influence your choice of clothes is a whopping mistake.

Any woman who thinks the fashion industry has her

interest at heart is woefully wrong. The industry is interested in her pocketbook. And it will sell her, often at inflated prices, anything that will make money for the industry. It will sell her shoddy merchandise, and it will sell her tacky styling—anything to keep the cash register ringing. Not only has the industry not gone out of its way to produce clothes that will help women get ahead, it has crammed down their throats garments that will most definitely hold women back.

In the last several years one of the major thrusts in the fashion industry has been clothes and accessories with designers' names or initials on them. Stores are bursting with designer items to the point where the concept of designer items has become a joke. Recently I noted in my newspaper column that a department store was selling Designer Dirt. A few weeks later I received a bag of the stuff in the mail. With it was a good-natured letter from a representative of the manufacturer explaining that the Designer Dirt idea was prompted by the fact that the practice of putting designers' initials on everything had reached absurd proportions.

A designer's name on a garment is no guarantee that the designer created or even looked at it before it was produced. What it does mean is that the designer is going to get a piece of the action. In return, he or she is usually selling you a piece of failure cloth with a big price tag.

And there is plenty of evidence that it does fail. We tested the effect of women wearing or carrying designer items in the office. The reaction of other women was mixed. About one-third responded favorably, and the other two-thirds had either a neutral or a negative reaction. Of the men, 90 percent reacted negatively. They treated the women who wore or carried the designer items as lightweights, and they assumed that these women were more interested in form than substance.

There are several reasons why designer clothing fails for the American businesswoman. One is that many of the leading designers are European by birth or by training. As such, they are products of an in-group that is conditioned by European society. Their views do not square with the goals of American women.

American women want to get ahead. They want to sit in the boardroom and in the president's chair. And they are heading in that direction. In 1976, one-third of the master of business administration graduates of the top American business schools were women. The M.B.A. is the union card for the executive elite of the American business world. So in ten years American business *should* have a large number of women at the top. In France, however, male executives dismiss the idea of women entering the executive elite as ludicrous. They treat such a notion as a silly American idea that will be short-lived. The concept of a woman with serious executive ambitions is also anathema to many Italians. The head of one Italian company told me that every executive office in his company had a couch. He said the only way a woman would get into one of those offices was on the couch.

A society in which the people in power are intent on keeping women barefoot, pregnant, and as far from the boardroom as possible cannot design clothes for women who have serious executive ambitions. The fact that the fashion industry's big number of the mid-1970s was the peasant dress, often made with yards of taffeta, shows how out of step the fashion industry really is.

The American designers miss from another direction. Until about fifteen years ago the idea of becoming a top fashion designer was not a popular goal of talented American men. Very few American designers, men or women, had made it big. There was no family or corporate network in which aspiring top designers could progress from heirs apparent to leaders. The Europeans had a lock on the field. So the Americans who made it hauled themselves up by their own bootstraps (which probably were not initialed).

Most of the American bootstrap types who have made it to the top have lower middle class backgrounds. Even though they brag today about their association with the beautiful people, they reflect their own lower middle class backgrounds in the clothing they design.

So while the Europeans design clothes that will keep you at home, the Americans are churning out garments that will keep you in the secretarial pool.

Obviously, some designers do a better job than others. It is also true that clothes designed by Americans generally test far better than the Europeans' clothes. So any woman working in a standard corporation who buys a European design is paying a lot of money for failure.

An examination of the designers' allegiances helps put the situation in perspective. When Ralph Nader attacked General Motors, he attacked the design of cars. At no point in the exchanges between GM and Nader did the car designers pretend that they were working for the public. They tacitly acknowledged that they worked for GM. When I attack fashion designers, however, they act as if they don't work for the manufacturer. They claim they work for the public. That is, of course, nonsense.

Just as auto designers work for General Motors, fashion designers work for manufacturers. True, clothing designers work for several manufacturers, but the relationship is essentially the same. They design basically what the manufacturer wants to produce. Therefore, they are tied in more closely with the manufacturer than they are with the consumer. If they really worked for the public, they would design reasonably priced, durable garments with as little built-in obsolescence as possible. And they would design and promote clothes that would help women get ahead.

It is not surprising that when I applied scientific methods to the selection of clothing and developed wardrobe engineering, fashion designers, manufacturers, and others attacked my approach. They have put forth all the classic arguments that are aimed at stopping progress.

The first is "Since you don't agree with us, you're an outsider, and therefore you have no right to disagree with us." That's the old circle within a circle.

The second is "We've been doing this for years and years, and therefore it is right." The world is still flat.

The third is "We'll ignore you, and you'll go away." I have no plans to "go away."

Wardrobe engineering is here to stay.

BEDROOM OR BOARDROOM—YOUR CHOICE

Despite the rhetoric of the feminist movement, many women, including businesswomen, continue to view themselves as sex objects. Sexuality is certainly an important part of our lives. But when sexuality is a factor in choosing business wear, it harms a woman's career.

Unfortunately, our testing proves that dressing to succeed in business and dressing to be sexually attractive are almost mutually exclusive. Except for very rare situations, you can't do both at the same time. Most men don't try, and those who do try fail, at least in business.

In past centuries and throughout much of this century, women were indeed primarily considered sex objects. That was partly because men subjugated them and partly because they let themselves be subjugated. But women are no longer the cardboard characters that appeared in the early novels of Enlightenment England. They have depth and personality. They have career goals that they are determined to reach. Nevertheless, many women still cling to the conscious or subconscious belief that the only feminine way of competing is to compete as a sex object and that following fashion trends is one of the best ways to win.

It's not.

DOES YOUR BACKGROUND HURT YOU?

Women must overcome socioeconomic barriers when they choose their clothes.

Today hundreds of thousands of women whose parents never went to college are going to college themselves. They're getting training and degrees that will point them toward the power ranks of American society. But in order to move in, they must do more than arm themselves with degrees and training. They must learn the manners and mores of the inner circle. And the inner circle is most emphatically upper middle class.

Someone who said she lived on "Toity-toid Street" or who said "He don't" or "We seen" would immediately be categorized by almost any woman with a college degree as lower class and incapable of holding an executive position. Yet, when compared to the style of the inner circle, many of these educated women dress "Toity-toid Street."

We have twenty-twenty vision when we look down the social scale. Most of us speak better than "Toity-toid Street," and most high school and college graduates don't say "He don't." We can immediately recognize the imperfection of such speech. But the people who say "Toity-toid" or "We seen" don't hear themselves speaking any differently from anyone else. We are myopic when we look up the social scale.

The same is true of nonverbal communicants that have social significance, such as clothing.

Somehow the people who know "the right thing" to do immediately recognize everyone who is doing it wrong. But the people who are doing it wrong never see themselves as being any different.

This book will help any woman whose background keeps her from choosing the right clothes.

RESEARCH, NOT GUESSWORK

Seventeen years ago I was an English teacher in a prep school in Connecticut. I needed money, and I told the director that I was about to quit. To encourage me to stay, he helped me get a summer job in a government project. Every morning I taught youngsters to read, and in the afternoon I conducted an independent research project.

I was assigned the topic of teachers' clothing and its effect in the classroom. My research on that topic resulted in several fascinating conclusions. Among them were these:

• The color, pattern, and cut of a teacher's clothes affect the attitude, attention span, and conduct of high school and junior high school students. For example, I concluded that a woman teaching in a lower middle class neighborhood could wear a "Persian rug" pattern in her dress and still be effective. In an upper middle class suburban area, the students would tune her out.

• An outfit can be one teacher's salvation and another's downfall. Women in their forties and fifties wearing soft, feminine clothes impressed students as authoritative mother figures. But young women in similar clothes had trouble controlling classes. To be effective, their style had to be starker.

Before that research project, clothes were only things I threw on in the morning to protect me from the elements. But that project shifted the focus of my professional life from teaching adolescents how to use language effectively to teaching adults how to use clothing effectively.

While I was still teaching, I began to do clothing research part-time. Some law firms learned about my research on teachers and hired me to find out what clothes could increase lawyers' credibility with judges and juries.

Lawyers steered me to politicians who were looking for an edge with voters. I made some politicians look so believable that I actually believed they would pay the bills I sent them. I should have known better.

Soon I started building a clientele of big corporations, which did pay.

Companies would call me in to solve specific problems.

"Should the tellers in our bank wear uniforms?"

"Our company is moving to Arizona. How should our executives dress?"

"The guys in one of our departments dress like Bowery bums. How can we spruce them up?"

"We have an outstanding employee we want to promote, but she doesn't dress the part. Can you help?"

"Our salespeople are cleaning up in big cities, but we can't crack small towns. What's the problem?"

To solve many of these problems, I had to set up research projects. Frequently I used employees of client companies as subjects and sometimes as researchers. I gathered as I sowed. And for the past seventeen years I have been compiling a data bank on the effect of just about every article of clothing imaginable.

My clients now include important political figures in the United States and abroad, numerous Fortune 500 corporations, and influential private individuals.

I have helped many men and women in their careers, and I believe I have succeeded where others failed because I have never based my advice on my own opinion. I have based it exclusively on research.

It was a harsh reality that forced me to rely so heavily on research. The reality was that my opinion was not valid. When I first got into clothing research on my own, I ran out and bought twelve suits. As soon as I started doing the research, I realized that my lower middle class background had conditioned me to buy the wrong suits. I gave eight of them away, and if I had been a little richer and a little more honest with myself, I would have given away ten. With a track record like that, you can see why I didn't depend on my own judgment in giving advice.

The minute I mention research, I automatically put people on the defensive. They say to themselves, "Here's a man who's going to give us a myriad of statistics." Or they say, "Here's someone who is going to give us 'absolute truths' that may not be absolute." I am going to do neither.

What I am going to do, without boring you with tons of statistics, is present the results of nine years of research into women's clothes. My research cost several hundred thousand dollars. Most of the money was put up by major corporations.

I have not described in detail the methodology of my research, since that would require a second book of at least the same length. I would like to point out, however, that I used standard techniques and an experienced research team. This is the same organization that researched men's clothing.

In addition, I had the assistance of some of the finest

corporate researchers in America in setting up tests and in gathering and interpreting data. Their reliability and their testing instruments were beyond question. Since most of the work was carried on for major corporations at their expense, I was subject to their review, and they were tough overseers.

However, I was my own strict taskmaster. I accepted only predictive validity as an adequate measure of accuracy, even though this type of validity is most difficult to establish and most costly to attain.

Another reaction I get from women is that I will be a magician who will give them a look of success instantly and at little cost. I cannot do this. Women who wish to look successful must, at least in the early stages, spend quite a bit of money for clothing. But once they develop a successful wardrobe, it will be relatively inexpensive to maintain.

The corporations that financed my research on women's clothes did not put up all that money out of altruism. In most cases it was because they were being pressured by the federal government to move women into executive positions.

When the government started turning the screws, companies started setting up executive training programs for women. Some of the programs involved assertiveness training. The women were told to stand up for their rights, to tell off the boss if he sent them for coffee.

At one large corporation someone asked what I thought a woman should do if the boss sent her for coffee. My response was, "If you have to tell your boss not to send you for coffee, you must have already told him nonverbally that you were ready to go."

I went on to say that the problem was being approached from the wrong perspective.

Women who want to be taken seriously and who want to succeed must dress in a way that says, "I am important. I am a business professional and don't you dare send me for coffee!"

There were two extremely successful women in the room at the time. Both agreed with me. And they said the reason most young women wouldn't succeed was because they didn't look like they wanted to succeed.

SHOULD WOMEN IMITATE MEN?

Throughout the period that I researched women's clothes, I read every article I could find on how businesswomen should dress. Most were inaccurate, some were dangerous, and all were the product of guesswork.

These articles generally were based on one of two premises: that anything goes or that to get ahead in business, women should imitate men's clothes.

The "anything goes" articles were written by fashion industry types who were not going to put themselves in a straitjacket by saying that one item worked better than another. Next year the industry might decide to manufacture and sell the other.

Everything does not go. Certain industries require certain dress. And while there is nothing morally wrong with a polyester pantsuit, research shows that it will not help you in business. A good skirted suit says you are an upper middle class executive type, while an obviously cheap polyester pantsuit says you're not. My research shows that when you're wearing a good skirted suit, it is easier to give orders and have them carried out.

The people who write those kinds of articles try to counter that fact by saying such things as "Clothing doesn't make the woman." They assume that people who believe that clothing is important also blindly believe it is the only thing that counts. Of course, it is not. A woman needs drive, ambition, intelligence, and education to move up the executive ladder. Without those qualities the best clothing in the world won't do anything for her. But even with them, if she doesn't have the right clothing, she won't get ahead.

The "imitate men" advice usually came from women in industry. Their articles appeared in industry-oriented magazines. They tended to base their advice on their own experience. Their experience generally came down to "I don't know what else to do, so I'll imitate men around me." And they wore things like pinstriped suits with vests.

My research indicates that a three-piece pinstriped suit not only does not add to a woman's authority, it destroys it. It makes her look like an "imitation man," and that look always fails.

The "imitation man look" does not refer to looking tough or masculine. The effect is more like that of a small boy who dresses up in his father's clothing. He looks cute, not authoritative. Rather than making him look larger and more grown-up, the father's clothing only draws attention to his smallness and kiddishness. The same thing applies to women. When a woman wears certain clothes with male colors or patterns, her femaleness is accentuated. She frequently looks more diminutive. And this reduces her authority. My testing showed that some men find the "imitation man" look sexy. Other men are completely turned off by it. In either case a woman's authority is diminished.

This is a prime example of why research is necessary. Obviously those fashion designers who turn out "imitation man" clothes and call them career apparel are advancing only their own careers.

In some of the articles on women's clothes, the writers used material from my men's book, *Dress for Success*, as the

IMITATION MAN LOOK

Never wear—

    Man's fedora

    Shirt and tie

    Pinstriped or
    chalk-striped suit

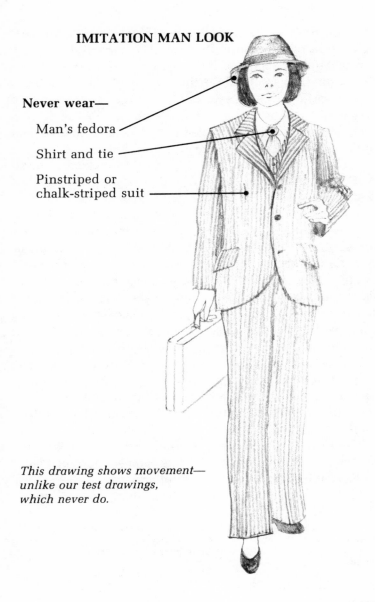

*This drawing shows movement—
unlike our test drawings,
which never do.*

basis for their advice. One article said women should wear beige raincoats because John Molloy proved that beige raincoats are upper middle class and black raincoats are lower middle class. I did say that. For men! I also said that a man wearing a beige raincoat would get better seats in restaurants, would be more likely to be obeyed by his secretary, and would be treated more like an executive than a man wearing a black raincoat.*

If I had been forced years ago to guess which raincoat works best for women, I also would have guessed beige. But that guess would have been, at best, incomplete.

My research showed that a woman wearing a black raincoat is definitely not automatically categorized as lower middle class. Raincoats are important for women, but not as important as they are for men. A woman can wear a raincoat of almost any color. If she wears a black raincoat, she will have a far stronger executive image than if she wears one of the salmon pink or dew forest green raincoats that are being sold, particularly if the black raincoat is made of a standard material and the others are made of shiny material.

The raincoat that tests best for women in both business and social situations happens to be beige. But it also happens to have a rich artificial or real fur collar that is about three inches wide and a fur lining. It should fall about three inches below the knee.

The second best raincoat for general use is black with a similar collar and lining. And this raincoat outranks beige raincoats that do not have such collars.

In the summer and in the Sun Belt, such coats are

---

*Some individuals and a few stores have invoked my name and have implied that they are affiliated with me or have access to my continuing research. I have not authorized or trained any speaker or consultant to represent me officially.

RAINWEAR

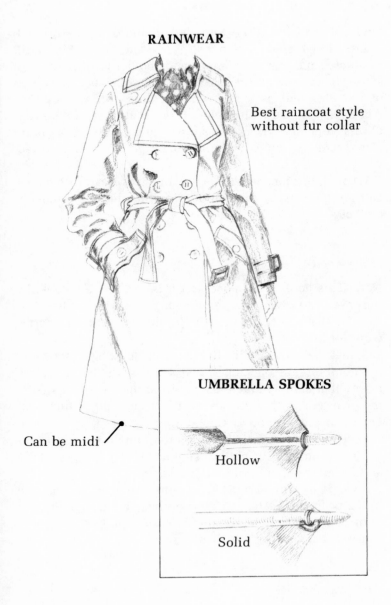

Best raincoat style
without fur collar

Can be midi

UMBRELLA SPOKES

Hollow

Solid

obviously too hot. (The Sun Belt includes the traditional South, New Mexico, Arizona, Nevada, and Texas. Missouri, Kentucky, and Maryland are considered borderline Sun Belt states. In the summer, Kansas City, Missouri, becomes part of the Sun Belt as far as which colors will work well.) Although any suitable colored raincoat that completely covers your skirt works, a simple beige midi works best. (This is one of only two midi-length garments that tested well.)

What all this means is that you can't use research on men's clothing as a basis for determining the effect of women's clothes.

SEXISM? NO!

Note: This book is designed as a classic "how to" book. Its purpose is to give every American woman a simple set of rules so that she can make her clothing and her accessories work for her.

Sometimes this specifically involves dressing to make the right impression on men. *This is not sexist.* It is a stark reality that men dominate the power structure—in business, in government, in education. I am not suggesting that women dress to impress men simply because they are men. My advice to women is based on the same principle as my advice to men: Your clothes should move you up socially and in business, not hold you back.

If women control a substantial hunk of the power structure in ten or fifteen years, I will write a book advising men how to dress in a female-dominated environment.

It is not sexism; it is realism.

Chapter 1

Instant Clothing Power
for the Businesswoman

Every woman in the United States has, at one time or another, been given second-class treatment simply because she is a woman. The list of people who give women short shrift is long. It includes hotel employees, store clerks, receptionists, telephone operators, doctors, and bureaucrats. Business people of both sexes are prime offenders. They simply do not take women as seriously as they take men. To the woman who does not work, all of this is annoying. To the business or professional woman, it is devastating.

The women's movement has given women more professional clout, but they still have a long, long way to go before they are on an equal footing with men. Legislation, governmental guidelines, and government pressure have made it a lot easier for women to get jobs. In fact, in many areas reverse discrimination has taken over, and women have a decided edge.

But as far as success on the job and opportunity for advancement go, the old prejudices are still enormous obstacles for women.

THE BUSINESS UNIFORM

There is one firm and dramatic step women can take toward professional equality with men. *They can adopt a business uniform.*

That is not a suggestion I casually put forth on the basis of a spur-of-the-moment notion. This suggestion is the product of years of laborious research involving thousands of men and women. That research led not only to the conclusion that businesswomen should adopt a uniform, but it also gave me more than ample information to spell out exactly what that uniform should be. A detailed explanation of the research for this project follows later in this chapter.

Like many of my research projects, this one came about almost accidentally. I had a luncheon appointment with three executives of a major corporation at a New York restaurant. I didn't know them or what their first names were. I only had the last name of one of them.

The appointment was for 12:30 P.M. I arrived five minutes early, looked around, and decided that since these executives obviously had not shown up yet, I'd have a drink at the bar. When I had them paged fifteen minutes later, I discovered to my embarrassment that they were sitting less than ten feet away. They were three of the best and most conservatively dressed women I had ever met, yet I had never considered the possibility that they might be my executives. I had been looking for three men.

When I apologized, they told me my reaction was normal. They said they always had trouble when they were away from the office. One said she was tempted to carry her desk plaque around with her. It said "VP SALES." They all agreed that their problem was especially acute when they traveled. At hotels and motels they felt particularly put upon. Desk clerks and porters seemed monumentally disinterested in accommodating them. One woman was particularly steamed up over the fact that when she traveled with her assistant, a man in his early thirties, he got preferential treatment every time.

It immediately occurred to me that her assistant had a sign that everyone could read. He undoubtedly wore a suit and tie, and that suit and tie said "Businessman." It occurred to me that the woman who made the facetious suggestion about carrying her VP SALES sign around with her had really hit on something. I came to the conclusion that there was a real need to develop a sign for business*women* to wear that is just as effective as the sign worn by business*men*.

I decided to explore that situation. My organization conducted a nationwide survey. The response showed that, indeed, there was no outfit that was widely regarded to be anything approaching a uniform for the business or professional woman.

Further research (described on pages 40–47) showed the following:

• There should be a uniform.
• Beyond any doubt the uniform should be a *skirted suit and blouse*. In most cases the suit should be dark and the blouse should contrast with the skirt and jacket.

This outfit will give businesswomen a look of authority, which is precisely what they need.

If women are to enjoy widespread success in all industries, they must adopt this uniform. It is their best hope.

One indication that the skirted suit will be widely adopted

is the fact that in some industries it already has been adopted. In banking and finance—particularly in the Wall Street area, which is the center of American business—few successful women would consider regularly wearing anything but the skirted suit.

When this uniform is accepted by large numbers of businesswomen, as I am confident it will be, it will be attacked ferociously by the enemies of women, many of whom are themselves women. The uniform issue will become an acid test to see which women are going to support other women in their executive ambitions.

The entire fashion industry is going to be alarmed at the prospect of women adopting a business uniform. They will see it as a threat to their domination over women.

And they will be right. If women adopt the uniform, and if they ignore the absurd, profit-motivated pronouncements of the fashion industry when they select their uniform, they will no longer be malleable. They will automatically and irrevocably break the hold that the male-dominated fashion industry has had over them.

If the work uniform is adopted, it will cut dramatically into the fashion industry's sales of both high-priced and low-priced garbage. So the industry should indeed feel threatened.

The fashion industry might use one of two methods to combat this threat.

First, they can use the industry's favorite ploy—the disappearing act. Whenever they don't want something on the market, they simply take it off. Poof! It's gone. That's what the industry does to any alternative to anything they are pushing at any given time. If they decide to do this with the skirted suit, they probably will leave unacceptable token elements of it on the market. That means suits selling for more than $350 and less than $60. But they can't do this without the cooperation of the retail establishment. If the fashion industry tries to take the skirted suit off the market, women should let out a loud, collective howl. And they should close their pocketbooks.

The other method the fashion industry might use to fight back is to start creating nothing but suits for women to wear on social occasions, in hopes that fashion groupies— and subsequently great numbers of other women—will start wearing suits to parties. Their objective would be to undermine the effect of the skirted suit as the business uniform.

If you are a businesswoman, you should *not* wear your skirted suit uniform for nonbusiness occasions. There are two reasons.

First, it really will undermine the effectiveness of your skirted suits as business uniforms. Men can get away with wearing their "uniform" on social occasions because everyone recognizes the suit and tie as primarily a business uniform. But the skirted suit has not yet been established as a women's business uniform. When the world has been preconditioned to think of it as such, women will have more leeway to wear it socially.

Secondly, my research shows that the skirted suit is not effective for social occasions. The suit gives you authority and a sense of presence in business. But that's not what most women want on social occasions. They want to be attractive and to have fun. Research shows that they are most likely to accomplish both wearing a dress.

The skirted suit, however, should become the uniform for almost all business and political situations. Women appearing on television should wear it. Leaders of the feminist movement should wear it, because in order for the women's movement to win, women must achieve equal status in their jobs. And they cannot have equal status and equal pay

DOING IT RIGHT

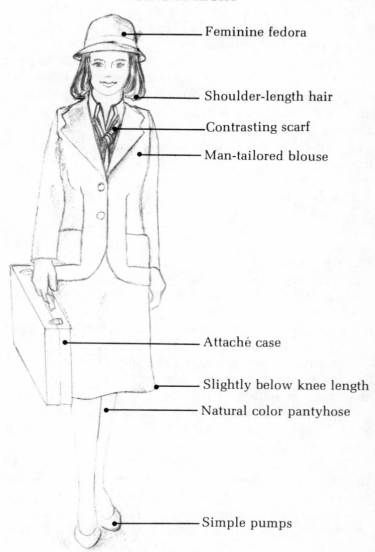

Feminine fedora

Shoulder-length hair

Contrasting scarf

Man-tailored blouse

Attaché case

Slightly below knee length

Natural color pantyhose

Simple pumps

DOING IT WRONG

Slouch hat

Ruffled blouse

Long hair

Button pulls,
indicating poor fit

Mismatched plaid

Jacket and skirt
do not match

Handbag

Midi length

Boots

without a collective image equal to that of men. Without a uniform there is no equality of image.

RESEARCH PROOF THAT THE UNIFORM WORKS

We waded into our research on the uniform concept confident that we'd have it all nailed down in several months. It took years.

Here is a condensed version of the steps in our study.

After determining that no executive uniform for women existed, we set out to identify which of the outfits being worn by women in business were the most likely candidates for the uniform.

We started by picking, with the help of my client corporations, 126 women in management positions. These women worked for 28 companies in 12 industries in every section of the country. They included vice-presidents of major corporations, women in politics, women who ran substantial businesses, women in middle management, and women in lower management jobs. For obvious reasons we excluded women in any job that required a uniform.

Our research teams were able to observe these women at work 1,240 times. During this observation period none of the women were aware they were being studied. (We verified this when we used these same women in a second study. One of the questions we put to them in the second study was "Have you ever taken part in a clothing study before?" They all answered no.)

According to what the women were wearing, this was the popularity ranking:

1. Conservatively cut dress
2. Tailored skirted suit
3. Tailored pantsuit
4. Skirt and blouse
5. Slacks and blouse

We suspect that many of the observations of the last two categories were actually observations of women who had removed their coats at work. We tested those outfits anyway, since they were functioning as business apparel.

Three facts prevented us from using the statistics from this original survey as a basis for deciding what the uniform should be.

First, we knew that the male-dominated fashion industry had conditioned women to buy failure clothing for their husbands. And we suspected that they might be doing the same terrible thing to themselves.

Second, although the dress was the garment most often worn by businesswomen, the dress did not represent a single look. It really represented several looks. Some of the looks paralleled the skirted suit, and others were quite informal.

Third, in some industries women had already adopted a uniform of sorts. It was the skirted suit in the male-dominated Wall Street firms and the pantsuit in the female-dominated firms on Madison Avenue.

Before testing whether a dress, a pantsuit, a skirted suit, or something else would work best as a business uniform for women, we had to determine which cuts, colors, and materials would be most effective with which particular groups, not just the general public. This turned out to be extremely complex. For example, one of our first discoveries was that one of the most effective authority *dresses* a woman could wear was gray pinstripe.

With this information in our pockets we ran out to test the gray pinstriped *suit* and found that it worked very poorly. Unlike men's business clothing, authority didn't necessarily transfer when you transferred the same color and pattern to a different type of garment. That meant that we had to test each garment separately. And that cost an extra $20,000.

We set up a four-stage procedure to find the ideal garment for the businesswoman.

Stage One

We enlisted a fashion designer to identify the basic designs in dresses, suits, skirts, and slacks. She made us swear never to mention her name. If we did, she said, she'd never again be able to work in the fashion industry. We then had an artist draw, under her supervision, a dozen variations of each design for each outfit. This team produced 646 pictures of dresses, 242 pictures of pantsuits, 256 pictures of skirted suits, 154 pictures of skirts, and 154 pictures of slacks, all on neuter figures. ("Neuter" in this context means lacking in characteristics that made them individualistic.)

We had each of the 1,452 sketches reproduced six times, bound in plastic, and passed out to each of six groups of researchers.

The research groups divided these numbered sketches into 56 sets of 25 and 2 sets of 26. The pictures were constantly shuffled by a computer so that every picture competed against every other picture at least three or four times.

Pictures were shown to five groups.

1. Male executives
2. Female executives
3. Male office workers
4. Female office workers
5. The general public

Each respondent was asked to close his or her eyes and envision a male executive. The respondent then was shown 25 pictures of men in various outfits and was asked to pick the one that came closest to his image of an executive. The almost unanimous choice was a man in an upper middle class suit, shirt, and tie. We did this to establish a precedent for the second question. We then had the same people close their eyes and picture a woman executive. Then we showed them the pictures of the women and had them pick the executive look.

Four months and 1,282 interviews later, we had our preliminary results.

Then we discovered that we would have to revamp the test. We learned that male executives' reactions frequently deviated considerably from the reactions of the other respondents.

For example, the total group response ranked the navy blue skirted suit and the navy blue highly tailored pantsuit as the most efficient garments in their categories. But male executives overwhelmingly chose the woman wearing a gray suit as the typical efficient executive. Since most businesswomen work in environments dominated by male executives, men are crucial to the success of businesswomen. So we had to sharply increase the number of male executives and virtually conduct a separate study of them.

We made one other major change. At first we accepted the fashion industry's definition of a skirted suit. That definition included a blazer with a coordinated skirt. But our initial test results indicated that those ensembles tested differently from the matching skirted suit. We found out that many businesswomen kept blazers in their offices and used them as instant authority ensembles with a skirt or dress. Therefore, the jacket had to be tested with skirts and with dresses.

Result of Stage One. This was the executive-impact ranking that our respondents gave the ensembles.

1. Skirted suit
2. Dress or skirt with a blazer
3. Dress with a matching jacket
4. Man-tailored pantsuit
5. Simple dress
6. Skirt and blouse
7. Slacks and blouse

8. Skirt and sweater
9. Slacks and sweater

Stage Two

The first thing we did in stage two was to eliminate those outfits that were never chosen. The purpose of stage two, then, was to find out not only what categories were performing best but to learn what variations of the outfits in the various categories tested best. So we had individual ensembles compete against each other.

Result of Stage Two. We cut the field to 36. That included the 30 top performers, all from the first 3 categories, and the top outfit from each of the bottom 6 categories.

Stage Three

The purpose of this stage was to get more detailed information on people who are important to the businesswoman and more detailed information on the garments.

We grouped the surviving 36 outfits into three sets of 12. Then we divided the male and female executives we were surveying into three categories, according to what kind of company they worked for: female-dominated companies, high fashion male-dominated companies, and traditional male-dominated companies. (We also continued to survey the "general public.")

Again, we sharply increased the number of male executives. Several corporate clients helped by supplying us with subjects. At this point we were really researching two things: the general effect of an executive uniform and the effect of an executive uniform on male executives.

Result of Stage Three. This survey reinforced the previous ones. The skirted suit was the odds-on favorite with the two groups that businesswomen had said were their problem groups—male executives and male office workers.

The skirted suit that worked best with the general public was navy blue and the skirted suit that worked best with executives was charcoal gray. Other outfits that tested well were a gray dress with a navy blazer, a gray pinstriped dress, a navy dress with a matching jacket, and a black skirt with a black silk blouse.

Note: It is at this point that most research on clothing stops. And it is exactly at this point that I believe real research begins. The results are convincing only when the clothes are tested in the environment in which they will be worn.

Stage Four

Over a four-year period we enlisted 347 women for our testing. Of those 347 women, 202 were in management jobs and 145 were competing for management jobs.

They agreed to wear 6 outfits picked randomly from the top 12 on 20 different days. At the end of each day they were to fill in a form with the following questions.

1. Today I was treated like an executive by my superior.
   Yes   No
2. Today I was treated like an executive by my co-workers.   Yes   No
3. Today I was treated like an executive by my subordinates.   Yes   No
4. Today I was treated like an executive by people in service capacities who are important to executives—waiters, taxi drivers, and so on.   Yes   No
5. Today my authority or my professional decision-making was challenged.   Yes   No
   If yes, by a male?   by a female?

Of the 347 women, 211 finished the test.

The dropouts quit for a variety of reasons. Several fell away simply because early on they discovered that the skirted suit worked best, and they weren't going to jeopardize their careers by wearing anything else for my research project.

Result of Stage Four. As a group, the women felt they were one and a half times as likely to be treated as executives when they were wearing the skirted suit.

Their authority was challenged 18 percent less frequently with a skirted suit than with any other outfit. The figure was about 32 percent when they were dealing with men. At first those two figures (18 and 32 percent) seemed out of line. But in follow-up interviews, the women indicated that they were more likely to be challenged by women but that they weren't worried as much about those challenges. The really serious challenges, they said, came from men. And that gave this result even more importance.

At the end of the testing period, we interviewed each of the 211 women and asked them, "Will you wear any one of the ensembles more often than any of the others?" Here was the result.

    1 was undecided

    1 chose the skirt and blouse

    2 chose the slacks and blouse

  10 chose the plain blue dress

  16 chose the tailored pantsuit

181 chose the skirted suit

That 181 of 211 picked the skirted suit was overwhelming proof, we thought, that the skirted suit was undoubtedly the best business uniform for women. We were convinced that it would work.

But later we got an unexpected chance to see that it did, indeed, work.

ONE COMPANY'S EXPERIENCE

A major corporation retained me to help solve a problem involving its women engineers. The corporation had done research that showed that its women engineers were less efficient when they were away from their home offices.

The problem was that these women had to identify themselves almost by name, rank, and serial number to all employees at a new site in order to get their cooperation. Even then, they didn't always get the cooperation, so they had to force the issue. It seems that people were just not used to responding to women as engineers. All of that adjustment at each site was time consuming.

The company wondered if there was a "uniform" that could help the women with their identification problem. I told them I was going to recommend one in this book but that none yet existed in the eyes of the general public. Company officials said they didn't want to wait until the book came out and asked if I could establish a uniform for their women engineers. I said I would give it a try.

There were 43 women engineers working out of seven major locations. When we brought them together and told them our intentions, the majority went along, although 13 of the women objected strenuously. But the company brass insisted that all of the women participate in this study.

From then on when any woman engineer left her home office, she wore either a gray or blue suit with an appropriate blouse and a simple pair of shoes. Within sixty days, the employees in the corporation had started doing three things.

1. Recognizing women engineers and responding to them as decision-makers.
2. Poking some fun at them.
3. Emulating them. Many of the secretaries started wearing versions of the same outfits, which usually were less expensive.

At the end of six months, company officials said there was still a difference in the performance of the women in the home office and in the field but that the difference had decreased. In our early discussions of the uniform, some corporate officials had expressed concern that women would quit in droves if they were forced into uniforms. At the six-month mark, just the opposite was true. The quitting rate was down.

Most of the women engineers enjoyed the prestige of having an executive uniform. Of the 13 who originally objected, 9 were now solid fans of the program.

At the end of a year there was no discernible difference between the women's performance at their home offices and in the field.

The company conducted a survey before the uniform and another survey one year after the uniform was adopted. The second survey showed that the general attitude of the women's bosses toward the women engineers had improved dramatically. And twice as many of the women than in the previous year were to be recommended for promotion.

A COMMITMENT

After that experience, the proof that a uniform was needed, and that this uniform should be the skirted suit, was so solid that I began advising women in my client corporations to adopt the skirted suit uniform.

In most cases the women took this advice seriously. At one corporation the women were particularly enthusiastic. One woman said, "Let's really plunge into this." She and two other women drafted a pledge and passed it around to other women in the firm. The pledge essentially read,

> I pledge to wear highly tailored, dark-colored, traditionally designed skirted suits whenever possible to the office, not to wear such outfits socially, and to encourage other women to do the same. I am doing this so that women may have as effective a work uniform as men and therefore be better able to compete on an equal footing.

I took a copy of their pledge, changed it slightly, and have since had many, many corporation women sign it.

Chapter 2

The Success Suit

If I had let my research stop with the conclusion that the skirted suit is the best outfit for a woman's business uniform, I could not have given businesswomen the specific information that my client corporations required—or that you require when you go out to buy a skirted suit.

THE RIGHT SKIRTED SUIT

In researching the particulars of the skirted suit and blouse ensemble, we used many of the same techniques described earlier in this book. We found the indirect question, computer-controlled, large-number survey particularly useful. The "indirect question" part of it means that we didn't come right out and ask subjects such questions as "What do you think of the suit the woman in this picture is wearing?" Instead, we would do such things as show them two pictures of the same woman with one variable—the suit, or the blouse, or whatever—and ask them such questions as "Which woman has the better job?"

In our testing of skirted suit ensembles, we surveyed more people than we did in the first seven years of our research on men's clothing.

This chapter, therefore, is the "postgraduate course" in the skirted suit as the woman's business uniform.

As I'm sure you realize, you don't want to rush out and buy the first skirted suit you see. Some cuts, colors, and patterns work; others don't. Some materials are better than others. And you must wear the right blouses with the right suits.

Cut

Our research indicates that the man-tailored blazer suit works best. Specifically, that means a jacket with a blazer cut and matching skirt.

The jacket should be cut fully enough to cover the contours of the bust. It should not be pinched in at the waist to exaggerate the bust.

The sleeves must be long.

This suit should be worn *without* a vest. Vests make women more sexually attractive and, therefore, less authoritative.

Although scarves are not an essential part of the uniform as a man's tie is to his uniform, they can be effective attention-getting devices. (The discussion of scarves is on page 77.)

Suits with skirts that fall just below the knee test best. Minis and midis come and go, but the most efficient business suits have not varied in length more than two inches in the last seven years. So if you buy one that's slightly below the knee, you should have a garment that will serve you for years. (This is one reason why if businesswomen adopt the skirted suit as a uniform, they will be taking a major step toward liberation from the fashion industry.)

Material

The materials that test best are wool and linen. Synthetics that accurately capture the feel and look of wool and linen work as well. I recommend them, although not as strongly as real wool and linen.

The synthetics and combinations of natural fabrics and synthetics travel very well. If you prefer natural fabrics even while you travel, I suggest tweeds. They look good even after three hours on a plane. For traveling in the South, I would recommend combinations of cotton and polyester that look like linen. Linen takes a beating when you travel.

Pattern

Only three patterns tested well.
1. Solids
2. Tweeds—or what I call the bushy British pattern (It's an indefinite pattern that virtually acts as a solid.)
3. Plaids
The plaids that work are not the exaggerated ice cream seller's plaid, but they are one or two degrees stronger than those in a man's business suit.

Women are not tied into as drab a look in suits as men. In fact, drabness is usually not as effective for women. The pinstripe, which is the high status symbol for men, is a strong negative in women's suits. It gives off the "imitation man" effect, particularly in pantsuits, and that look destroys a woman's authority with men.

Colors That Test Best

Please note. The color suggestions are based on thousands and thousands of hours of research. If they are not taken *exactly* as written, they will not have the desired effect.

The two colors that tested best in a solid-colored wool or linen suit are

> Gray that is two or three shades lighter than charcoal. (It's the average gray of a man's suit.)
> Medium-range blue (the average blue in a man's suit).

The other colors that tested very well are*

navy	steel gray
charcoal gray	dark brown
medium-range gray	beige
camel	deep maroon
black	deep rust

Tweed suits are multicolored. But the only tweed suits we were able to test were those with a dominant color. Tweed works well with these dominant colors:

> rust
> brown
> medium-range gray
> blue (ranging from medium to navy)

Tweed suits often have accent threads throughout the suit.
• If the dominant color is rust, the best accent thread is blue or deep brown.
• If gray is dominant, the best accent thread is blue.
• If brown is dominant, the best accent threads are beige or blue.

*The colors in this and other lists are not ranked in order of preference.

• If blue is dominant, the best accent threads are white or beige.

Those accent threads work well because by picking them up in the blouse, you form a psychologically more effective ensemble.

Plaids also are multicolored. They have three sets of colors in them:

1. A dominant color. (Sometimes there are two dominant colors, such as blue and gray.)
2. Accent colors.
3. Accent threads.

The following dominant colors test best in plaids.

navy	medium-range gray
gray (two shades lighter than charcoal)	blue-gray
	deep maroon
charcoal gray	rust

The following accent colors test best in plaids.

white	charcoal gray
black	navy
rust	medium-range blue
beige	tan
dark brown	

We were not able to test all combinations under all circumstances; therefore, I do not have information on accent threads in plaid.

Colors to Avoid

Avoid these colors for suits:

    most pastels, particularly pink and pale yellow
    most shades of green

mustard (Mustard tested so poorly that if someone gives
you a mustard suit, I suggest you burn it.)
bright red, bright orange, bright anything else
any shade that would be considered exotic.

If you show up at the office with an exotic color, you will
be the envy of the fashion fans you work with, but male
executives will not trust you. In general, stay away from
colors with names like sea mint green or salmon pink. At the
same time be aware that most advertising for women's
clothes is written to sell, not to describe the item. Sometimes
they give an exotic name to a standard color, so you might
have to see the item before rejecting it.

BLOUSES

Our research on blouses was as heavy as our research on
the suits themselves.

Your decisions on which blouses to wear with which suits
should not be emotional or aesthetic decisions, since the
blouse you put with the suit will make a measurable
difference in the psychological impact of the suit.

The blouses I am going to discuss will all be in solid
colors, not only because it would have been impossible to
test all the variations of patterns but because solids tested
best. (Plaid blouses also tested well for businesswomen's
suits.)

The solid blouses we tested worked best when they were
cotton or silk; however, you can go with any synthetic or any
combination of natural fiber and synthetic that looks like
cotton or silk.

The blouse should be simply cut, with no frills or lace.

The best neckline is the equivalent of having a man-
tailored shirt with one button open; the blouse collar may be
worn either inside or outside the coat.

BUSINESS BLOUSE STYLES

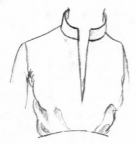

Neckline too low

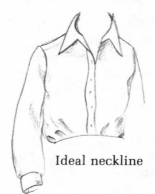

Ideal neckline

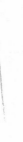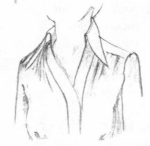

Too dressy

Lowest acceptable neckline

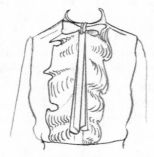

Too frilly

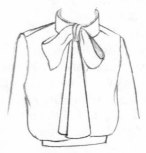

Acceptable nonfrilly style

How well blouse colors tested depended on several variables. Overall the best were the following:

white	medium blue
white on white	navy
pale yellow (not bright	cocoa
yellow)	dark brown
straw or pale beige	black
ecru	light gray
beige	pink (dark, bright, pale,
khaki	or end-on-end)
tan	orange
denim blue	Chinese red
light blue	maroon
end-on-end blue (this	rust
means there is a	pale green
certain texture in the	kelly green
material to add to the	gold
color)	salmon

EFFECTIVE COMBINATIONS

To drive home the point that you must take care when you combine suits and blouses, I will show the different effects of the first suit on the list (the gray) when combined with different blouses.

With the gray suit . . .

• a white blouse gives you very high authority, a high status rating, and a business executive image without offending even 1 percent of the male executive population.

• a black blouse increases your authority so much that you offend 15 percent to 20 percent of the executive population, particularly men over forty-five.

• a pale yellow blouse weakens your authority but increases your image of likability, credibility, and trust-worthiness.

• a maroon blouse gives you a high sense of presence.

• a light blue blouse softens you almost to the point where you have trouble being authoritative. A medium blue or an end-on-end blue softens you even further.

• a gray blouse destroys your authority, credibility, and upper middle class image. I don't know why, but it just works that way.

• a pale pink blouse will destroy your authority in some companies and enhance it in others. Pink and gray is a fine aesthetic combination, and it can give you authority if the people in the company are used to seeing men in authority with pink shirts. If they're not used to that, the pink blouse will lessen your authority.

There are hundreds of variations possible with each suit, and, therefore, I'm not going to list each of them separately. The three major areas in which the businesswoman should make her clothes count—authority, presence, and trust—are given in the following lists. Some of the suit and blouse combinations appear on more than one list. That simply means that that particular combination tested as being effective in more than one area; therefore, the categories are not mutually exclusive.

Authority Outfits

These combinations create a high authority image for a woman:

1. A solid gray suit . . . with a white blouse
   or with a white-on-white blouse
   with a pink man-tailored blouse
   in corporations where the men
   generally wear pink shirts.

2. A medium-range blue suit with a white blouse.
3. A navy blue suit . . . with a white blouse
    or with a white-on-white blouse
    with a gray blouse
    with a maroon blouse.
4. A charcoal gray suit with a white blouse
    or with a pink blouse in companies
    where pink shirts are worn
    regularly by the men.
5. A medium-range gray suit with a black blouse
    or with a white blouse.
6. A camel suit only with a deep blue blouse and only in the South.
7. A dark brown suit only with a white blouse and only in the Midwest.
8. A beige suit only with a deep blue blouse and only in the Sun Belt or in the summer.
9. A deep maroon suit with a white blouse
    or with a black blouse.
10. A deep rust suit. . . .with a black blouse
    or with a white blouse.
11. A black suit with a white blouse.
12. A steel gray suit. . . .with a white blouse
    or with a rust blouse.

None of the plaid suits rate as highly authoritative, so on any day that you have to bull your way through a difficult situation, you should stick with one of the suits on the above list.

Presence Outfits

Researchers have learned that if two six-footers and one person five feet six or shorter are in a closed environment and the discussion becomes heated, the two six-footers will start talking to each other and will ignore the shorter person, unless that person has a strong sense of presence. The sex of the short person is inconsequential unless it is a woman using sex as an attention-getting device. This is a problem for most businesswomen, who cannot be overtly sexy but must hold their own in heated discussions. Our studies indicate that the best nonsexual attention-getting device is color. Certain color combinations can give a woman this needed sense of presence.

The following suit and blouse ensembles tested best for a sense of presence:

1. A gray suit . . . . with a white blouse
   or with a rust blouse
   with a pink blouse
   with a maroon blouse
   with a black blouse.

2. A medium-range blue suit with a white blouse
   or with a dark blue blouse
   with a camel blouse
   with a beige blouse
   with a maroon blouse
   with a dark brown blouse
   with a deep rust blouse.

3. A navy blue suit . . . . with a white blouse
   or with a rust blouse
   with a medium-range gray blouse
   with a pale yellow blouse
   with a tan blouse
   with an orange blouse
   with a red blouse
   with a gold blouse.

4. A charcoal gray suit . . . . . with a white blouse
   or with a pink blouse.

5. A medium-range gray suit with a pink blouse.
6. A dark brown suit. . . . . . . with a white blouse
   or with a navy blouse
   with a light blue blouse
   with a rust blouse
   with a maroon blouse.
7. A beige suit with a navy blue blouse.
8. A black suit . . . . with a white blouse
   or with a black blouse.
9. A camel suit with a blue blouse (those shades of blue generally found in men's clothing).
10. A steel gray suit . . . . with a rust blouse
    or with a maroon blouse.

Believability Outfits

You have to be believed to be trusted. Women have a greater difficulty making other women believe them than they do men.

Therefore, our research in this area concentrated more heavily on women subjects than did the research in many other areas.

The ensembles in which you are most likely to be believed (by both men and women) are these:

1. A medium-range blue suit with a white blouse.
2. A navy blue suit with a white blouse
   or with a pale yellow blouse.
3. A medium-range gray suit with a medium-range blue blouse.
4. A deep maroon suit with a white blouse.
5. A deep rust suit with a white blouse.
6. A tan suit with a medium-range blue blouse.
7. A beige suit with a medium-range blue blouse.
8. A camel suit with a medium-range blue blouse.

Popularity Outfits

Everybody in corporate America knows that it can help you to find someone higher up in the corporation who will help you up—a sponsor. This can be tricky for a woman because if she attaches herself to a man with a higher corporate rank, the attachment often appears sexual. There is another unfortunate fact: Women complain frequently that other women do not help them. And women have to overcome those two obstacles.

To get a sponsor, you first have to be liked by that person. You will be liked or disliked more on your mannerisms and your attitude than on the way you dress. But your clothes can help. Our research shows that if you wear certain colors, you will appear to be in a bright, cheery mood, and if you appear to be in a bright, cheery mood most of the time, you are much more likely to be liked by both men and women.

The colors are simple: a blue and pale yellow combination, or a beige (or tan or camel) and blue combination. Any time you wear a blue suit with a pale yellow blouse or a beige suit with medium or light blue blouse, you can sit at your desk and beam at everyone, and they'll think you're blissfully happy—while you're planning to take over the company.

Chapter 3

Packaging Yourself

Everything a woman wears sends a message.

Although we spent more time researching the skirted suit than any other garment, we have researched every major item worn or carried by women. In addition we tested such elements of style as hair and makeup, such behavior as the use of liquor for business meals, and such trappings of the business world as office furnishings. Most of these are discussed in this chapter.

We employed a variety of research techniques. It was necessary to test each item individually and in multiple-item studies. For this report I have synthesized the multiple-item and single-item studies.

In this section, whenever I am discussing the function of, or reactions to, an item strictly in a social (nonbusiness) context, I will specify.

Here is my report, item by item.

Dresses

In this book the skirted suit has stolen the thunder of the dress. In a way that's too bad because the dress is the centerpiece of the woman's wardrobe.

My research team has conducted dozens of studies on dresses. We not only showed pictures of women in various dresses to men and other women, but we also did extensive testing in which women wore the dresses in various environments.

One example is the sleeve test. We gave four women four dresses each. The dresses were almost identical in style and color. Each woman got a long-sleeved dress, a dress with three-quarter sleeves, a short-sleeved dress, and a sleeveless dress.

These four women, product consultants for a major corporation, conducted training sessions for retail people all over the country. In the test they were to report on the reactions of the people they were training and also on the treatment they got in restaurants and hotels.

Very early in the test it became clear that only long-sleeved dresses worked almost everywhere. It was about three months before we realized that the three-quarter-length sleeve worked in most of the Sun Belt. This was surprising because in a preliminary survey there was no indication that that length would be accepted in the Sun Belt. What this proves is that two-dimensional photos or drawings do not always test three-dimensional reality.

The dress is the most versatile garment a woman can have, for the dress can be anything from sportswear to formal wear. A dress can say "I'm in charge," and it can say "I'm available."

Certain dresses have a higher authority rating than many skirted suits. The strongest is the gray pinstriped dress.

But the dress is more subject to the whims of fashion than the skirted suit. Dress lengths, for example, go up and down more than the length of skirted suits. This is one reason why I am not suggesting dresses for the business uniform.* Another reason is that the dress can be the ultimate seduction garment. It is the outfit in which men find women most alluring. And sexual attraction detracts from authority.

This discussion of dresses will be limited to those that are likely to be worn on an everyday basis.

From a socioeconomic standpoint the dress is a difficult item to buy.

If you are from the lower middle class, no matter how long you have been in the money, you should avoid dresses with too much flounce or flourish and stick to conservative, well-tailored dresses for which you have cross-shopped very carefully. (Cross-shopping is explained under the section How to Cross-shop, page 171.) Patterned dresses almost always tip off background, so unless you have a very strong feeling for what clothing is upper socioeconomic, you should avoid all new patterns and stick with traditional ones.

These are the dress colors that tested best for the office:

deep blue	gray
navy	medium-range blue
tan	light gray
beige	rust
dark brown	

---

*The main reason is the overwhelming result of the research described in chapter 2.

These colors of dresses tested poorly for the office:

green	purple
orange	baby blue
light rust	pink
bright yellow	bright red
lavender	

The following colors tested as being most appealing to men:

pale yellow	black
beige	white
pale pink	rust
pink	tan
navy	red

These colors turned men off:

gray	orange
green	lavender
bright yellow	mustard

Since navy, rust, and beige scored well both for business wear and for attracting men, those are good dress colors to wear to work on days when you're going to meet a man right after work.

The colors mentioned above were tested mainly in solids for two reasons.

1. It was practical. It would have cost several hundred thousand dollars to test all the variations of colors and patterns of women's dresses, and by the time we finished, the results could have become obsolete.

2. Solids work best on most occasions.

There are, however, other patterns that test well. In the office, the pinstripe, the chalk stripe, and plaids (particularly in gray or blue or combinations of the two) work quite well.

Businesswomen can also get away with wearing paisleys, windowpane, and such traditional checks as houndstooth.

Businesswomen cannot get away with wearing feminine prints with flowers, birds, sail boats, and the like. Many of the abstract prints should also be avoided. Although most of those prints are perfectly acceptable to wear socially, they will make men think that a businesswoman wearing them to work is frilly and ineffective. The pattern that tested worst was floral. I would even advise against wearing it socially.

Here are a few more points on dresses.

• A dress with a jacket is effective for the businesswoman. Matching dress jackets test well. Blazers that contrast with a dress give authority to the wearer and test best.

• Dresses made of any material that clings, shines, or makes noise when you walk tested as unsuitable for office-wear.

• Any dress that has a halter top or requires any second piece on top is also unsuitable.

• Any dress made of sporty material, such as denim or corduroy, is not for work.

• In summer women have always worn light and brightly colored dresses to the office. Do this only if you wish to be or remain a secretary.

You can wear lightweight materials.

The summer colors make a woman appear ineffective. We found that the women wearing the light summer colors, particularly in dresses, had twice as many authority problems in the summer as they did the rest of the year, when they weren't wearing those colors. This finding applies particularly to the Deep South, where summer colors are worn year round. We discovered that Southern women found it far more difficult to function in authority positions than women in the North.

DRESSES
Two dresses that tested well

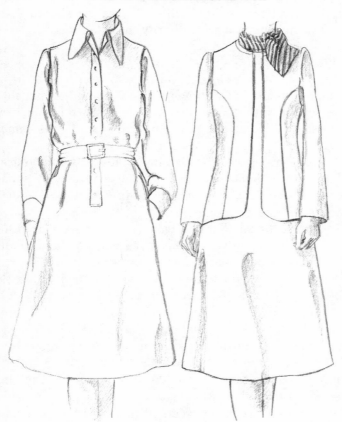

Simple shirtwaist   Dress with matching jacket
SUCCESS DRESS PATTERNS FOR THE OFFICE

Solid   Plaid   Stripe

67

I recommend that you wear only dark-colored dresses to the office—if you're going to wear a dress at all. You can wear lighter-colored skirted suits because the skirted suit usually carries much more authority than the dress.

Skirts

A couple of decades ago, if you called a woman a "skirt," it was a left-handed compliment. It was telling her that she was a sexpot, but it was also cutting away some of her dignity. I found that the skirt can still give off the same message.

We took pictures of 12 women in various skirt and blouse combinations and showed them to 100 executives. (To each man we showed pictures of only one woman.) We asked them to guess the corporate position of the woman.

Sixty-one guessed that the woman was a secretary, 30 guessed she was a typist, and 9 guessed that she did general clerical work. Not one guessed that she was an executive or a professional or that she was on an executive track.

Obviously, for the businesswoman a skirt is a flag of failure. Incidentally, women who take off their jackets when wearing a skirted suit are then wearing a skirt and blouse.

Only one skirt and blouse combination tested relatively well. That was a black skirt and a black silk blouse. But that is not the type of blouse you could put under a skirted suit to make the skirted suit most effective.

Skirts, however, can be excellent items for the nonbusinesswoman. They function beautifully in many social situations, and they hold up well under the abuses of travel.

Here are some tips on skirts.

• The best skirts are wool or have the look of wool. In skirts, the country-tweed look is very upper middle class and highly recommended.

• Linen or the look of linen will work in the South or in the North in summer. A good winter skirt should be fully lined. And the material of the lining should match the skirt. You don't want to wave a red flag from under your hem.

• An ample hem is the sign of a good skirt. Skimpy material means skimpy workmanship. With an ample hem, you can raise or lower the skirt as you wish, although only with some materials can you lower the hemline. (I hope women soon free themselves forever from the yoyo-like length pronouncements of the fashion industry and settle on lengths at or close to the knee.)

• A skirt should have a reinforced waist. If it doesn't, it looks baggy.

• The zipper should always be concealed in the seam, and it should be the same color as the fabric. If you can see the zipper, it's a cheap skirt.

• Every woman should have a long, flowing skirt. I recommend black for most areas, white for the South. It can be worn with a simple blouse for a formal occasion. If you're going out of town and you're not sure whether you will be going to any dress-up gatherings, you can wrap this skirt up in a little ball and pack it. In an emergency you can wear it with any number of blouses and get away with it for several nights. It is the best traveling formal ensemble available.

Blazers

Any garment that's been around for decades even though the fashion industry doesn't push it is apt to be a very good buy.

Not only has the blazer been on the scene for a long time, but it also will last a long time as a workhorse of your wardrobe. That's why the fashion industry is unenthusiastic about it; you won't have to buy a new one every time you turn around.

The blazer is, by its very nature, upper middle class. Every woman should have at least one. If you are a businesswoman who often wears dresses to work, you should have at least three blazers. The first two would be for work only. They should be, or look like, rich wool. One should be camel colored; the other should be navy. All you have to do is put one on over a dress of a contrasting color, and you have instant authority. The third should be strictly for social occasions. It can break all the rules of the business jacket. It can be a tweed, herringbone weave, multicolor check, plaid, or anything similar. It can have leather patches on the pockets and elbows, leather buttons, or anything that has the flavor of the English countryside.

Here's what to do when you're shopping for a blazer.

1. Cross-shop (particularly if your background is lower middle class).
2. Reject anything that looks cheap. Always reject obvious polyester.
3. Give it the grab test. Grab the sleeve and wrinkle it. If it doesn't fall out without wrinkles, find another blazer.
4. Try it on and button it. The shoulders should fit snugly, but there must be enough play to move your arms around.
5. Check the cut in a multiple mirror. The blazer must cover, not accentuate, the contours of your body. It should cover your bust, and your rear shouldn't stick out too much.
6. Look at the collar and lapels. They must lie flat and cling to the contour of the neck. The lapels should roll and not look like creased paper. Peek under the collar and make sure that the underside has been reinforced. Make sure the stitching on the inside is small and even.

7. Inspect the lining. The stitching should be small; the lines should be even. For office wear, the color of the lining should blend in with the other fabric. You must avoid contrast. A bright yellow lining inside a dark blue jacket is a disaster.
8. If the buttons are unusual, demand extra buttons.

Small women note: A woman who is less than five feet two inches and under 120 pounds looks more effective in a blazer suit or a blazer and a dress than in any other set of garments *except* a strong-patterned plaid skirted suit.

Pants

The fashion industry is constantly trying to talk women out of pants and into dresses. It's a lost cause. Women know the comfort of slacks, and they're going to wear them.

I always found women in pants ultrasexy. But so many people told me otherwise that I was starting to think I might be a little weird. I'm happy to report that our research shows I'm normal and that my reaction is standard. Most men find women in pants very sexy. They're not attracted to women who look as if their pants have been sprayed on nor to women whose build is extremely large. The women who are least attractive in pants are the ones the fashion industry puts in them—thin, reedy women who don't have enough natural padding to wear them well. But pants on the average well-rounded woman are widely acclaimed to be a hit.

Well-tailored pants are one of the great triumphs of the clothing industry. For women on a tight budget, they are a must. Pants are particularly good for young mothers and homemakers, since they climb ladders, chase children, pick up rocks, dig in gardens, vacuum rugs, and crawl under beds. Rough, durable material, such as denim or corduroy, is best for jobs like that. Polyester is not good; much of it snags.

Dressier slacks—good wools and gabardines—make excellent informal wear. They're ideal for shopping or walking on a cold day. They are standard gear for upper middle class women at informal gatherings.

When you go to buy slacks, shop with care.

If you don't recognize the material, run a grab test on it. Grab the material and crush it. If it falls wrinkle free, it's cleared one hurdle. Then compare the material with several other pieces of material and see if it looks rich. Don't try on a pair of slacks unless it has passed both of those tests.

When you're checking slacks, always start at the top. If the waist has to be taken in more than an inch and a half, forget it. Since you're going to pay for the tailoring, it will cost too much and be too tricky.

Make sure there is ample hip room. If the slacks are not cut for you, don't take them with the idea that the tailor can adjust them. It won't work.

Then check the drape of the slacks. Roll up the cuffs, look in a mirror, and make sure there is no sagging or bagging.

Have the tailor make the pants break over the front of the shoe and slope neatly toward the back.

At this point you should have slacks that fit snugly (but not too snugly) in the hips, waist, and seat. The legs should fall perfectly without puckering, and the pants should break nicely on top of the shoe.

Do not assume that everything will fall miraculously into place if you go to a quality store. The executive wives we surveyed bought their slacks at the very best stores. But 14 percent of the slacks in their closets did not fit at all. It had nothing to do with their gaining or losing weight. There were flaws that were built into the pants from the beginning.

Pantsuits

In most business offices the pantsuit is a failure outfit. Testing showed it to be extremely ineffective when the wearer is dealing with men. The most common pantsuit, the polyester knit, will even kill your effectiveness with women. You can get away with well-tailored pantsuits in female-dominated companies. But you're taking a chance. If you have to deal with men, even as subordinates, you're putting on trouble. I advise against wearing them.

But since my experience as a consultant has taught me that some women will never give up this garment, I felt obliged to test which colors are most effective.

Navy blue, gray, charcoal gray, beige, deep maroon, rust, camel, and tan test fairly well.

Coats

The coat a woman wears telegraphs her status and affects her sex appeal.

Is sending a status message important? Consider this discovery we made in the course of our research: Although most men will deny it with their last macho breath, it seems that the first thing they notice about a woman is her socioeconomic level. We ran a series of tests in which we gave men only fleeting glances of various women who were walking past windows or through revolving doors.

We asked the men to guess at the women's jobs and educational levels, which they did with great accuracy.

We then asked them to tell us what the women looked like. In the vast majority of cases, they could not. They did not have time to register an accurate picture. They only received impressions that happened to include an accurate assessment of the status of each woman.

Since the coat is sometimes the only major garment that's showing, you should choose your coats very carefully.

If you're going to buy only one winter coat, my advice is that it be camel colored and a wraparound. That is the only coat that tested well at giving a woman both authority and appeal. A woman wearing it will be considered a social and business success. (The single exception is a woman who is

BEST WINTER COAT

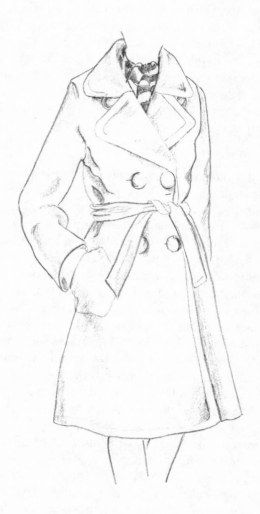

Camel-colored wraparound

more than 20 percent overweight. She should also avoid double-breasted coats and stick with single-breasted coats.)

I met with a group of executive women in a round-table discussion. They felt that a businesswoman should have several winter coats. Among their favorites were a medium-gray chesterfield; a dark blue, black, or deep-brown double-breasted coat with a belt in the back, and an earth-toned tweed.

Research indicates that you must avoid any coat that pinches at the waist, such as the princess, or any coat that is too dressy or suggests evening wear.

A woman wearing a coat with a large fur collar (larger or more conspicuous than that of the beige raincoat which tested well) or a fur coat will find it difficult to carry on a serious conversation with a male executive. These men tend to think that women in furs are feminine, frilly, and flighty—but not sexy. (Other coats that tested as unsexy were fake furs, heavy tweeds, and, on short women, heavy wool midis.)

On social occasions, however, the fur coat, especially the mink, could be an excellent choice for the executive wife. It says, "My husband and I are well-established members of the upper middle class." In some circles the right fur is a must uniform for the executive wife.

But fur coats have a very strong built-in negative. Approximately 6 percent of the American population is opposed to wearing furs of any kind on ecological grounds. And about half of those people, or 3 percent, will think less of anyone who wears fur. Those 3 percent are more important than their numbers suggest, since they are likely to be well educated and to come from moneyed backgrounds.

One powerful executive in a major corporation told me that he distrusts women who wear fur coats. He contends that anyone who wears fur in this enlightened age is either cruel, stupid, or a weakling who follows fashion and should be treated accordingly. His reaction is not unique, so I recommend that women never wear fur coats for business. You can wear your mink on social occasions, but when the event is both social and business, avoid fur unless you have met the other people.

Any cloth coat that is flattering and made of rich wool or looks as if it's made of rich wool will suit your purpose better than fur.

There are several styling details on coats that you must be careful to avoid. Extra pockets, gaudy buttons, buckles, or anything that appears added to the coat will usually make it lower middle class.

Also important, of course, is length. One of the primary rules of coat wearing is that the coat should completely cover the dress. That's hard to do with a floor-length dress, but even then the coat should come almost to the bottom.

We tested a beautifully dressed woman in a full-length evening gown with three coats that were identical in every detail except length. We walked her past three groups of 20 people attending a company affair at the Crown Center Hotel in Kansas City. We asked them to guess at her husband's position in the company. For the first group she wore a knee-length coat. Only two people guessed that she was the wife of an executive. For the second group she wore a midi, and six pegged her as an executive's wife. At that point we thought our woman probably looked too young to be married to an executive, but we ran the last section of the test anyway, since it had already been set up. To our surprise, inches counted a lot more than years. When she wore a full-length coat for the third group, 17 of the 20 guessed that she was Mrs. Executive.

Since the results were so surprising, we repeated this test in different forms. The statistics weren't always that overwhelming, and sometimes the midi even tested best. But generally the rule held up—so much so that one of the researchers dubbed the knee-length coat with long dress "the peasant formal."

Sweaters

Sweaters in the office spell secretary. Any woman at any level who wants to move up should not wear a sweater to work. In the office sweaters give out nothing but negative impulses. They say lower middle class and loser. If it's cold in the office, wear a warm blazer.

But for attracting men, no garment tests better than the sweater if it's tight and made of soft luxuriant wool. A cashmere sweater on a woman with even a moderate build is one of the greatest seduction garments in existence.

Vests

Don't wear a vest for business, particularly one that accentuates the contours of the body. Research indicates that when a woman wears a vest, she draws attention to her bust. With most women this is sexy, and with a busty woman it is very sexy. However, on small-busted women the vest can be an effective part of the business uniform.

On social occasions when you are interested in being appealing, the vest (any type, tailored or sweater) is a very effective garment. It registers as sexiest when it is tight and in a different color than the suit. Many businesswomen who have sat in on my lectures now don their contrasting vests at the end of the business day.

Scarves

A leading contender for the world's biggest rip-off is the abundance of scarves with designers' names on them that sell for three or more times what they should sell for.

It is particularly absurd for a businesswoman to wear such

SCARVES
Styles that tested best

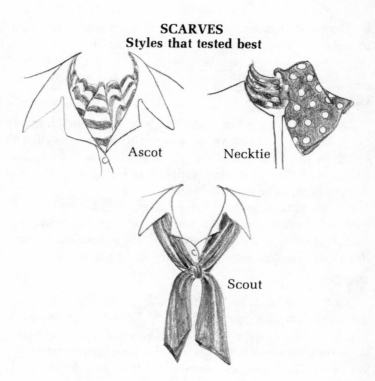

Ascot

Necktie

Scout

Patterns that tested best

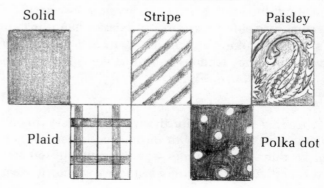

Solid

Stripe

Paisley

Plaid

Polka dot

a scarf. For a woman who works in a male-dominated environment, these scarves are not status symbols. They are, at best, neutral. With some men they will reduce your status. High-quality men's clothing seldom carries a designer label, and it rarely carries a designer label where it can be seen.

The best scarves are silk. The next best are polyester scarves that look like silk. Never buy an acetate scarf.

And remember: You don't need a designer's name on a silk scarf. Silk is made by worms, not leeches.

Shoes

The best shoe for a businesswoman is the plain pump, in a dark color, with closed toe and heel. The heel should be about an inch and a half.

The colors that test best for office wear are blue, black, deep brown, and gray. Testing fairly well were deep maroon, beige, and tan. All multicolored or brightly colored shoes flunk. Boots should not be worn to work.

American women have five times as many foot problems as men. That's because they're wearing trash on their feet. Generally that is not the fault of the American shoe manufacturers, many of whom are being forced out of business. Shiploads of women's shoes have been pouring in from Brazil and the Philippines, where they often were produced by fourteen- and fifteen-year-olds. The quality is low, they seldom have arches, and the lasts aren't quite suited to the American foot.

Two groups are getting rich on this: the retailers who are marking up the shoes as much as 150 percent (compared to the traditional 50 percent with the American-made shoe) and the foot doctors.

Two groups are taking a beating: the women who are being crippled and the workers in the shoe industry in the United States who are being laid off. I suggest that these two groups team up and force retailers to do something. Pressure from both ends would work.

One additional note: The towering platform shoe is the most preposterous thing manufactured for a woman since the chastity belt.

Pantyhose

Wear only skin-colored pantyhose. Anything else at work is unthinkable. Furthermore, anything else turns off men. All the non-skin-colored stockings tested so horribly that I don't even think they'd make an effective mask for a bank robber.

You should keep an extra pair of pantyhose in your desk in case the pair you have on gets ruined.

Hats

If women today want the world to take off its hat to them, they would be better off if they kept their own hats on. For a man or a woman a hat is a traditional symbol of power, authority, and position. A hat, particularly the right hat, adds height and substance to the wearer.

We all are familiar with the picture of the pleading peasant, hat in hand, standing before a nobleman or the contrite schoolboy, hat in hand, standing before the headmaster. Taking off your hat has always been a sign of submission, so it is ironic that women have chosen this moment in history to go hatless.

Women's hats serve two functions: They decorate a woman and they add to her sense of presence. As decorative items, like most supposedly nonfunctional items, hats act primarily as indicators of rank. They indicate the social, economic, and educational position of the wearer.

We placed researchers outside of exclusive stores and in front of budget department stores. They recorded the number of types of hats worn by women coming out of the stores.

HATS

Test well for business

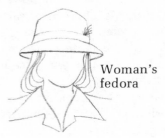

Brimmed
hat

Woman's
fedora

Test well for social occasions

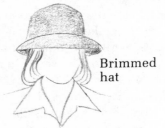

Cartwheel

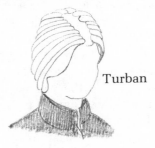

Turban

Do not test well

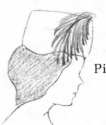

Pillbox

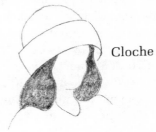

Cloche

81

The women walking out of the better stores were four times more likely to be wearing a hat than those coming from the budget stores. In addition, they favored different styles. Fedoras, picture hats, cartwheel hats, and other hats with brims were almost exclusively worn by the women coming out of the more expensive stores, while the nonbrimmed hats, with the one exception of the turban, were almost always the property of the other group. The bargain-basement women favored halos and pillboxes. The only brimmed hat that showed up on their heads with any regularity was the cloche, which has a modest brim.

A second experiment rounded out the hat picture. We had an artist draw twenty female faces. Then we showed them to various groups of people. We asked them to pick the richest, the smartest, the poorest, the sexiest, the meanest, the homeliest, and so on. Whenever subjects are asked to pick which of twenty faces have various traits, there usually are three or four faces that aren't chosen. Those are "neuter" faces. And that's what we wanted. We knew that after the artist added hats to the neuter faces and we showed them to the same subjects, the subjects would make their choices only on the basis of the effect of the hats, since the hats would be the only variable.

We put three different hats—large brim, moderate brim, and no brim—on a series of neuter faces. We asked the respondents to guess at the social status, corporate rank, and competence of the hat wearers. In every case, the larger the brim the higher the social status. However, in the other categories—corporate rank and competence—the hats with moderate brims tested best. Therefore, the hat that would work best for most businesswomen is a medium-brim fedora.

One word of caution. If the fedora looks masculine, it will reduce your authority. I suggest a maroon fedora with a little feather since men don't wear those.

Gloves

For the businesswoman, leather. Period. Deep brown is by far the best, and black and gray are acceptable. All other colors test poorly.

If you are dressing to be attractive to men rather than to have authority among them, knit gloves are an asset. Leather, kidskin, or anything else is all right, but the knits give you a softer, more feminine look. And the tighter the glove the sexier the glove, so don't go out and buy a first baseman's mitt.

When you're buying gloves for warmth, remember that your fingers get cold a lot sooner than the rest of your hand. Some gloves are lined everywhere except the fingers, so be sure you get a pair that is totally lined.

No young lady over age ten should wear mittens.

Hair

The first thing a woman must realize about her hair is that she has to wear it all the time. An extraordinary hairstyle is going to work only with extraordinary clothing. Since hair must work on different occasions and in different environments, every woman should have her hair designed to do just that.

My research showed that hairstyle is one area where a businesswoman has some leeway. But there are some rules.

I suggest that every woman go to a well-known hairstylist. You'll probably have to wait several weeks or months to get an appointment with Pierre the Expensive, but be patient: it's worth it. Most of these stylists with reputations are excellent. If you live in a small or medium-sized town where such virtuosos don't exist, take a vacation to a big city. It might cost you some time and money, but, again, it's worth the price.

If you are a businesswoman, tell the hairstylist that:

• Your hair must be medium length. What's medium? Well, it can never be so short or styled in such a way that it would look mannish or boyish. It must be fuller and longer than that. But it can't be any longer than shoulder length.

When Delilah cut Samson's hair, he lost his power. If women cut their hair too short, they do the same thing to themselves. Women with very short hair and with very long hair can be very feminine, very sexy, very appealing—and very nonauthoritative. If a woman wants to be authoritative, she must have hair in the medium range I described above.

• Your hair must lie neatly in place without constant attention.

• Your hair must not be excessively curly or wavy. If the current fashion trend calls for curls and waves, forget it. Too many curls and waves will hurt you in business.

If Pierre the Expensive does your hair right, and you like it, you should be set for a long, long time. You won't have to make any radical changes, although you occasionally might want to tamper with it slightly to fit in with some particular outfit or place you will be visiting. If you absolutely must have an exotic hairstyle for some specific occasion, get a wig.

After Pierre finishes, you might want to have some pictures taken of your new all-purpose hairstyle. Have it photographed from the front, side, and back. Then, when it's time to have your hair cut again, you can take the photos to your neighborhood stylist, who charges considerably less than Pierre, and tell him, "just like in the pictures."

Women have been dyeing their hair for thousands of years for a variety of reasons. The main two seem to be to look young and to look beautiful. My research adds a couple more—to gain authority and to keep from losing it. A businesswoman might think about getting rid of any gray. Gray hair adds authority to a man and takes it away from a

HAIRSTYLES
Test well for the businesswoman

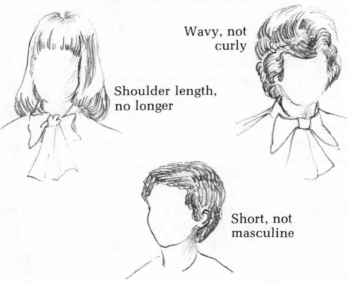

Wavy, not
curly

Shoulder length,
no longer

Short, not
masculine

Test poorly for the businesswoman

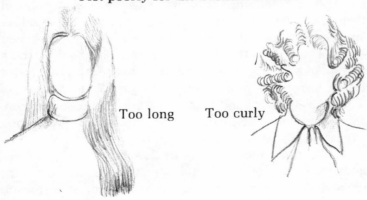

Too long   Too curly

woman. And, while blondes may or may not have more fun, brunettes definitely have more authority. Dark hair means power and blonde hair means popularity. So any cute, small blonde reading this book may want to decide whether she'd rather have more fun or more power.

However, you might also want to keep a sharp eye on all the newspaper and magazine reports on the dangers of dyeing your hair.

All exotic things done to hair are absolutely wrong. They make you look unauthoritative *and* unsexy. Tipping, streaking, and frosting all tested as being unsexy, lower class, and unauthoritative.

Makeup

The only performers who wear obvious makeup are circus clowns. All the world loves a clown, but men don't date them, hire them, promote them, or buy anything from them.

Makeup works best with men when they don't know you're wearing it.

We had six women ranging in age from eighteen to forty—all of whom were considered by co-workers and friends to to be good at using makeup—apply what they considered minimum makeup. Then we photographed them. Next, we sent them to expensive Fifth Avenue salons and had them get the works. And we photographed them again. Then we performed a twin test. We showed men a picture of a woman in the light makeup and a picture of her in the heavy, but professional, makeup. We told them the women were twins and that they were to choose the more appealing twin. The pictures each man looked at were of a woman who was about his own age.

Of 100 men under age twenty-five, 92 picked the minimum makeup picture. So did 67 percent of the men ages twenty-five to thirty-five. And 62 percent of the men from thirty-five to forty-five favored the minimum. So in most cases, when you pay for a makeup job, you're paying to drive men off.

We could have had these women apply the heavy makeup themselves. But we thought that by sending them to experts, we would be giving the cosmetics a fairer chance. But the makeup still took a beating.

The guiding principle for makeup is "Enough is enough and usually too much."

The exception is with women over forty-five. We ran a series of tests with this group also, and more than 92 percent of the men favored the picture of the woman who had been made up by the beauty expert.

The obvious conclusion is that most women in their twenties and early thirties should avoid makeup artists, cosmetics counters, and other puff and powder traps. That does not apply to women older than forty-five.

The guidelines for a businesswoman are more stringent than they are for the nonworking woman.

We gathered together nine women, all of whom have been executives for several years and all of whom are now training young women to become executives. In a round-table discussion, they came up with the following makeup guidelines:

• If you are under thirty-five, wear lipstick and little else. You should not use lipstick that stands out in any way. If fashion says everyone is to wear dark lipstick, wait until everyone is wearing it before you do.

• Obvious eye shadow is out. Six of the women at the table had been told by male executives that they object to a female candidate for promotion who is wearing eye shadow. For every male who states his objections, they all agreed there are five or ten men who don't.

• Eyeliner is also out.

• Long fingernails and false eyelashes are for actresses.

• Colorless nail polish only.

• Mascara must be used with great discretion. If it runs, it ruins.

• If you have already plucked your eyebrows, keep the line as natural as possible.

• If you have pale eyebrows, darken them slightly with a pencil. Pale eyebrows give the face a washed-out, weak look, and our research shows that a woman with that look lacks authority. This is particularly important if the woman does not wear glasses.

Perfume. The rules for perfume are simple. If you want to appeal to men, make it delicate and expensive. If you want to be an executive and men know you're wearing it, you're wearing too much.

Suntans. The sun can do three things: increase your sex appeal (many men find a tan attractive), increase your authority (having a tan is part of the executive mystique), and (according to medical research) increase your chances of getting skin cancer.

Glasses

After reading a research report on glasses, a woman in a corporation I consult for looked up at me and said, "Damn it. I've got twenty-twenty vision."

She had just discovered that our research indicates that glasses—the right glasses—add weight to a woman's face and consequently make her look considerably more authoritative.

I have seen small, ineffective women gain effectiveness simply by wearing windowpanes with proper frames. I've never recommended that to a client, but I know it works.

The right glasses have plastic or bone frames of moderate

size. The frames should match the woman's hair *if she is a brunette*. If she is a blonde or a redhead, she should not have anything in her glasses that picks up the tint of her hair. Her frames should be a dark, unaesthetic brown. Avoid wire rims.

For the same reason that glasses work very well for the businesswoman, they're a poor idea for the woman who is trying to be appealing. Glasses make her more authoritative, and there is a direct reverse correlation between authority and appeal.

I advise women who wear glasses to wear contact lenses socially and to wear conventional glasses for business.

Women should avoid sunglasses or any other glasses with shading, no matter how popular, fashionable, or chic they become. Testing indicates you won't be trusted or liked on business or social occasions if you wear shaded glasses. And I stress in spades that women should never pay a designer for his name on glasses, particularly those with shading, because that name plus the extra cost of making oversize lenses can add one-third to the price of the glasses—and without doing anything for the wearer.

Designer glasses, those big monstrosities women put on their faces, do the exact opposite of what they're supposed to do. They're supposed to make women attractive. Instead, they add weight to a woman's face; they add to her authority (although not nearly as much as traditional glasses); and, as a result, they diminish her appeal.

Jewelry

All the jewelry we tested, except pieces that were obviously cheap, tested well.

We held a round-table discussion with a dozen wives of executives. They came up with one major suggestion for young wives: while they are young, have their husbands buy them *better* pieces of jewelry. I laughed, but they insisted they were serious.

One woman said that every year on her birthday her husband bought her a little piece of jewelry. On their anniversary, he'd bring home another trinket. As a result she has a drawerful of insignificant jewelry she can't use. In the circle she moves in today, a very small, inexpensive cocktail ring is not appropriate gear for parties, nor is it sporty enough for the tennis court.

She and several of the other women said they wished they had headed their husbands off. They wish they had said, "If you're going to buy me jewelry, please don't buy me any for my birthday, for Valentine's Day, or Mother's Day. Put the money aside and get me *one* nice piece for Christmas." If their husbands had done that, they would have a hefty storehouse of jewelry they could still be wearing.

The same advice, of course, applies for women buying their own jewelry. Instead of buying four or five cheaper pieces throughout the year, they should buy one good piece.

Two of these women had another regret. Early in their marriage they had sold jewelry that had been left to them by their mothers. They thought the items looked dated. Both of them now wished they had had them remade because the stones and the gold are worth a fortune.

It seems that wives of executives need and thrive on jewelry, particularly when they jump suddenly to a higher socioeconomic level. You can go out and buy clothing, and you can go out and get a new car, but it's difficult to justify an expense of several thousand dollars to have immediately all the jewelry you think you need.

Diamonds, or any other jewelry, can be your worst enemy. The wife of one New York executive came from a family that had been in the diamond business for generations. As a result she had more diamonds than kids have marbles. When her diamonds lit up parties in New York and when she wore them to company headquarters, nobody thought twice about them. They knew her husband and they knew her family background. Everything went along fine until her husband was promoted to second-in-command of a plant in the Midwest.

When the couple arrived in town, the local executives and their wives threw a party for them. Diamond Lil, thinking it appropriate, trotted out her very best rocks. Mistake. The locals, including the wife of the number one man, didn't go for all that glitter. Apparently they thought it was a front or gauche or heavy-handed, or maybe they were plain old jealous.

The husband said that that was the first of many problems he had in the job. He emphasized that it got him off to a bad start.

He moved to another company and is now doing better than he ever could have done with the first. The lesson to be learned is, If you have expensive jewelry, don't wear it on the first meeting. Sneak up on people with it. Otherwise it will have the effect of artillery.

The most useful piece of jewelry any businesswoman can wear is a wedding ring. All the executive women we talked to agreed that a wedding ring announces to the world that they are there for business and nothing else. One highly successful executive wears a wedding ring even though she's not married.

The jewelry guideline for the businesswoman is simple: The less jewelry she wears, the better off she is.

If she wears any jewelry at all, it should be functional or should add presence. A large, expensive pendant can add presence to a small woman.

A watch should be extreme, almost a small version of a

man's watch. A ring shouldn't be a big bulge but should lie flat against the hand. A good guideline is not more than one ring at a time for business. A woman whose ears are pierced should wear simple gold posts. Dangling earrings are out. Anything that clangs, bangs, or jangles should be avoided.

Umbrellas

The average businesswoman can carry any good quality umbrella that has no gaudy or frilly touches. But most umbrellas are junk and fall apart because they are designed to fall apart. One clue to the quality of an umbrella is the number of spokes—a good one has ten or more. The best umbrellas have solid spokes (see drawing, page 31) rather than hollow ones. Unfortunately, most women's umbrellas are made with the hollow spokes, and they fall apart with the first puff of wind.

If you can't find a sturdy umbrella, at least pick one that's big enough. Fortunately, recent fashion trends have made it possible for a woman to buy an umbrella that's large enough to keep the rain off. That's particularly important for the businesswoman who travels from building to building. She can't show up disheveled or drenched. If you buy the kind that folds up, you should get one that opens and closes automatically, or you'll get soaked while you're opening or closing the thing.

There seems to be an unwritten code among some women that rain washes away all the rules. This belief can do nothing but harm them in business. Men keep their shoes shined and their ties in place on rainy days. But women who nine days out of ten look acceptable show up on a rainy day looking like refugees. They wear ponchos, rain shawls, little plastic rain hats, and all sorts of cheap, junky items. We've tested these items, and they all say "file clerk." If you wear them on a rainy day, people may remember you in your rainy-day garb when promotion day comes around.

Pens

All businesswomen should carry a pen, a pencil, or both. Carry only gold (or, if you're in the habit of losing pens, silver). I recommend the Cross pen only because it tests best. Under no circumstances should a businesswoman use a cheap pen or pencil in front of anyone else, even if the people she is dealing with are using cheapies themselves.

Attaché Cases

An attaché case is an indispensable item for the business-woman. Attaché cases are symbols of authority, and virtually every female executive totes one. If you see a woman in the Wall Street area without one, you can almost guarantee that she isn't an executive. Women's attitude toward the attaché case is one thing that has given me hope that they will adopt a uniform because so many have adopted that one part of it.

When I first started telling women to carry attaché cases, I addressed a group that included a woman who has a management job at a Wall Street brokerage firm. After the session she said, "John, I like most of what you say, but I'm not going to carry five or ten pounds of leather full of junk."

In my talk I had pointed out that some male executives carry their attaché cases even when they don't have any papers or other business paraphernalia to carry. Some carry only their lunch in the case; others carry their cases empty. But they wouldn't be seen without one. My Wall Street friend assured me that she was going to carry her case only when she had work to take home. If she ever carried it when her work didn't dictate that she had to, she said, she would buy me lunch. But she warned me not to look forward to that lunch because it simply wasn't going to happen. And that was that.

About three years later, when I arrived to do some work for

the company, she came up to me and said, "John, I'm going to buy you that lunch I owe you." She reminded me of our conversation and told me about an experience she had had two weeks earlier. She had been stuck in a New York subway during a fire. After an hour and a half she came out, gasping for air, looking like a chimney sweep and dragging her attaché case behind her. When she got up onto the street, there were 80 or 100 people waiting, trying to get a cab to get out of there. She walked down to the corner and spotted someone getting out of a cab, so she piled in. The driver turned around and said, "Get out, lady. I'm not taking you." She was about to get out when he looked back at her again and said, "Okay, I'll take you." As they rode along toward her apartment, she asked him, "Why did you decide to take me after you said you wouldn't?" And he said, "Look, lady. I'm not crazy. I'm not going to mess with any broad that carries an attaché case."

She now carries her attaché case every day. It's dark brown leather. It's plain, simple, and functional, with no decoration or hardware, the kind that tests best.

Handbags

It's better for a businesswoman not to carry a handbag. If you do carry one, it should be leather and of high quality. By the way, some of the very expensive designer bags are made of plastic.

Wallets

Businesswomen should carry wallets of dark brown leather or natural color leather only. Wallets should be made of good leather with no design or doodads and preferably should match or coordinate with your purse.

Women should be very careful when they take out their wallets after a business lunch. We ran a small test to learn what female habits annoy male executives. One such trait was fumbling through their handbags when they were to pay for lunch. Men don't object at all to women paying; in fact some of them enjoy it. It's making such a fuss over it that seems to annoy them. So I would suggest that you keep your wallet on top and your credit card in a place in your wallet that's easily accessible.

Incidentally, any woman who is an executive, or wants to act like one, must have a credit card. I recommend two: an American Express card and one of the bank cards—either Visa or Master Charge.

Credit cards are also very useful for women who are taking clients to lunch. One of the problems women complain about is that waiters and waitresses constantly present the check to their male guests. The credit card is an effective trump card for overcoming that. If, before the check is brought, a woman takes out her credit card and lays it next to her on the table in plain sight of the waiter or waitress, she'll probably be presented with the check. If you don't think that the card was spotted, just tap it once or twice on the table. If that, too, fails, leave little or no tip, and tell the waiter or waitress why. Next time it will be remembered.

Luggage

There is only one type of luggage any woman in America should carry. It is a matched set of canvas luggage with belting leather strapping.

If a woman carries belting leather luggage, which is the standard luggage of the male executive, she comes on as an imitation male. But if a woman carries pink, yellow, or other gaily colored bags that announce to the world that she is frilly, she will not get the best treatment. Those bags tell bellboys she is a nontipping secretary on vacation.

The luggage that tested best—good canvas with belting

leather strapping—received salutes from male executives and service from bellboys. The Louis Vuitton luggage tested better than all the rest. Close imitations without designer initials at half the price tested almost as well, and I would recommend them. The only places designer luggage had any positive impact were some of the top hotels in New York and one or two in San Francisco. In the rest of the country the people handling the luggage didn't recognize it, and the other locals weren't impressed.

One useful device is a business-card holder that functions as a luggage tag. These identify you as a business person. They create the impression you're going to tip. And they can be effective security devices. Some enterprising house burglars go to airports and look at the baggage tags of people leaving town. They copy down the name and address of the person and pay your home a midnight visit. A second-story worker can get your name off a business card but not your address.

Any woman who travels frequently and has to take a lot of luggage must feel like Sisyphus. Porters and bellhops are extinct at a lot of airports, hotels, and motels, so a woman can't avoid a certain amount of pushing, pulling, and lifting of luggage. But it really isn't necessary. I know women who have one or two big pieces of luggage with wheels or rollers. They can simply stand up the suitcases, pull out a strap, and roll them away.

If you are a saleswoman who has to carry heavy samples, ask your boss for a sample case with wheels. Tell your boss about a research project we carried out in 1974 with women selling office machinery. They had to carry in a rather heavy piece of equipment. Our researchers discovered that when the saleswomen walked in straining and sweating, it took them twice as long to get past the secretaries. In addition, they looked and felt bedraggled, and, as a result, rushed their

ACCESSORIES
Test well for the businesswoman

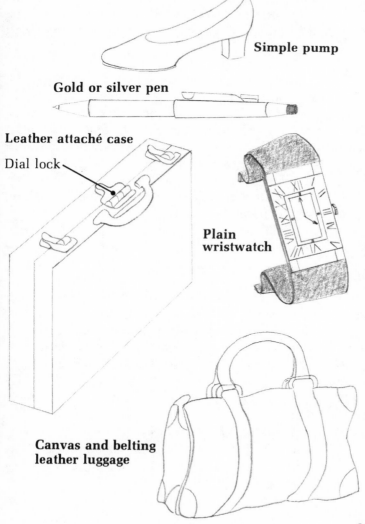

Simple pump

Gold or silver pen

Leather attaché case

Dial lock

Plain wristwatch

Canvas and belting leather luggage

sales presentations. And they didn't sell on a par with the men.

By putting the item on a piece of luggage that had rollers and a strap, we eliminated most of the negatives, and the women's sales increased dramatically; that means that if you strain and sweat carrying it in, you're less likely to carry it off.

Liquor

Boozers are losers.

We ran a series of surveys on the attitudes of men and other women toward women drinking. In general, the most liberal attitude was that a businesswoman could sip sherry or white wine. Thirty-five percent of the people think women should never drink. But women who don't drink but make it obvious that they object to other people drinking drew an equally negative reaction.

So if you drink, don't drink boilermakers or martinis. Stick with mild stuff.

Offices

There are all sorts of pitfalls a woman should avoid in her office. Here are some guidelines.

• Don't have your office painted anything but a standard office color. Blue and beige are the most widely used.

• Don't have a flower on your desk. It's the badge of a secretary.

• It's a good idea to keep extra sets of clothes in your office, but keep them out of sight.

• Although men display pictures of their wives, you should not have your husband's picture on your desk. That tested negatively. But pictures of children seem to be acceptable.

• Make sure your chair isn't so huge that it overwhelms you, makes you look diminutive, and detracts from your authority.

• Your ashtrays should be smaller than those in men's offices. You have to walk a careful line in decorating your office. It must be businesslike, but not masculine.

• Any paintings should be sexless. A painting of a cavalry charge or a steam locomotive would probably be too masculine; a watercolor of a meadow with a lot of pastels might be too feminine. Hang only neuter art.

• If your name is on the door, Mary Smith is much better than Mrs. Mary Smith, which tests better than Ms. Mary Smith, which in turn tests better than Miss Mary Smith.

Lingerie

If you want to be a liberated woman, burn your polyester pantsuit, not your bra. The polyester pantsuit will keep you in corporate serfdom, while your bra can help you up as well as hold you up. There's only one lingerie rule for the businesswoman: Wear bras that hold your breasts in place and hide your nipples.

Lingerie has always been sold as sexual packaging by companies that are more dedicated to sales than sex. They have never displayed much interest in finding out what lingerie makes women sexy. One thing they have tested, however, is which shades sell best. So that's what they make and sell.

One exception in the industry is a small California company that makes peekaboo and brightly colored lingerie. Although most of the items look rather cheap, our tests indicate that this small company produces sexier underwear than the major producers.

The sexiest look was found to be the high contrast look. A

woman with very white skin wearing black or bright red lingerie would be very sexy. A woman with a deep tan will look sexy in a white bathing suit. Undergarments or bathing suits can also make a woman sexy if they enhance the color of her skin. A pink bathing suit, for example, might give a pale woman a little bit of color. But the wrong lingerie or bathing suit will make a pale woman look like a corpse, and unless her man is an unusual fellow, this is not sexy.

The sexiest color in lingerie, according to our tests, is red. The next sexiest is black, but only on white women. The sexiest on black women is red, and the second sexiest is pale pink.

Lingerie that is designed to approximate skin tones, although widely marketed, tests as unsexy. Also unsexy is anything in gray or teal blue.

There are, however, so many variations of skin tone that it is impossible to give advice that works for everyone.

Lace is sexy. It's the only upper middle class peekaboo element in lingerie. And, it seems, the lacier the better. The frillier the better. The more peekaboo the better.

One additional thing that can make lingerie sexy is the element of surprise. In all the testing we did, red lingerie tested as the sexiest. However, when we showed men pictures of ten women in red lingerie and then a woman in blue, green, or almost any other color, they chose the woman in the unusual color as the sexiest. Therefore, it's probably a good idea to have ten sets of lingerie in different colors and to wear something different every night. That would drive a husband crazy . . . or, if the price of lingerie doesn't come down, drive the couple to the poorhouse.

Sportswear

For tennis, stick with the white dress.

Golf is still the favorite game of male executives. A lot of important business is transacted on the golf course. When businessmen go to a convention or seminar at a resort, they wheel and deal while they're playing golf. This freezes a lot of women out. Golf lessons would be a worthwhile investment for any woman who wants to get to the top of a big corporation. You don't have to become good enough to win the Masters, but if you are a horrible duffer, don't set foot on the course.

The other game you have to play on the golf course is the clothing game. Businessmen have a standard golf look: a pair of leisure pants and usually one of those shirts with an alligator on it. The major mistake women make is to clutter themselves with golf doodads. They tend to buy every little accessory in the pro shop. Too many of those make you look like a rube. Wear a golf skirt and a blouse with an action back and golf shoes. You can wear golf gloves and a golf hat, but no more accessories. On a cool day you can wear a light nylon jacket. Avoid sweaters.

If you're going to take up horseback riding, I suggest that you get the right outfit. That means pants with padding inside.

For skiing, simply go to a ski shop and buy the recommended items.

For boating or yachting, wear sneakers with nonskid bottoms. Denim outfits are a good bet. So are good cotton shirts in light pastels.

For any pool, lake, or beach affair that is business-oriented, wear one-piece bathing suits. Otherwise, if you have a good figure, two-piece suits will do just fine.

Be sure to get a high-quality swimsuit cover-up for walking to and from the beach or pool. I have not tested swimsuit cover-ups, so I can't recommend specifics. I would advise, however, that you go to the best store in town and spend some money.

Resort-wear is important to the businesswoman. Companies spend a lot of money sending their people to training sessions, seminars, and other think sessions at resort hotels and conference centers. The men dress casually, tending toward short-sleeved shirts, plaid pants, and soft shoes. They can sometimes get away with being gaudy, but women cannot. Their outfits have to be more subdued. Dark colors, especially maroon and navy, are best.

Some don'ts for training sessions and other company functions held at resorts:

- Don't wear feminine colors, such as pink and pale yellow.
- Don't wear lower middle class colors, such as purple and gold.
- Don't wear anything sheer.
- Don't wear silk, velvet, velour, or any material that is shiny or too soft.
- Don't wear pants; you're better off in skirts.
- Don't wear busy patterns. Avoid any pattern that looks like it belongs on a rug.
- Don't buy cheap stuff. This is one area where you can't skimp. Go to the best stores and pay top dollar.

Materials

Broadcloth. Standard material in men's shirting, excellent for women's blouses.

Camel's hair. Best winter coat material for most women. Wraparound with tie best style.

Cashmere. Great for sweaters that will keep you poor but sexy.

Corduroy. Excellent for sportswear. Should never be worn for business.

Cotton. It breathes, it wears, and it succeeds. Unfortunately, it also wrinkles.

ACTION SPORTSWEAR

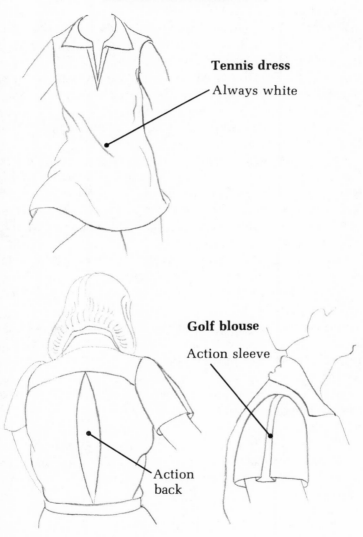

Tennis dress

Always white

Golf blouse

Action sleeve

Action
back

Crepe. Standard in a little black dress. Afternoon only, never to business.

Denim. Excellent upper middle class sportswear—the blue work shirt look, which means you don't work with your hands. All denim is good, except at work.

Foulard. Tie silk, associated with "Daddy went to Yale" pattern. Excellent in scarves for businesswomen. Also excellent in dresses for the executive wife.

Gabardine. Best when it is made in texturized polyester. Otherwise it wrinkles too easily.

Lace. The most feminine and sexiest of all materials. Lace dresses test as one of the sexiest and most appealing types of all dresses. Lace trimmings on lingerie also have high sex appeal. For all the above reasons, lace should never be worn to the office, nor for any occasion when you want to exert authority.

Leather. Only in shoes, gloves, handbags, and attaché cases to work. And no imitation leather.

Nylon. Some blouses are excellent and easy care. Good for traveling.

Polyester. Tough, durable, easy-care material. Only useful when texturized. If it looks like polyester, it says "peasant." Never wear a polyester knit. (Any other knit should also be avoided for work.)

Satin. Always acceptable for evening wear. Tests best when it's luxurious and heavy.

Shantung. Never wear it to work.

Silk. Says rich, successful, and sometimes says sexy.

Suede. A standard upper middle class material often acceptable for business wear, always acceptable for social wear.

Tweed. Excellent for suits.

Velvet. A thick, soft, pile material that says sexy.

Wool. A fine, soft upper middle class look. Great for suits.

Cities

There is a certain sameness to a lot of American cities. Standardization has been upon us for years. Franchised hamburger stands and familiar motels ring the outskirts of all cities, and the downtowns are generally a combination of blocky-old and sleek-new buildings. But underneath that sameness there are distinct local speech patterns and municipal idiosyncrasies in dressing and in people's reaction to clothes.

In our years of testing, we have uncovered many of these local peculiarities. We have also researched how clothes fare in different neighborhoods of various cities, and we learned, not surprisingly, that what works on the South Side might torpedo you on the West Side. Here are some municipal characteristics.

Atlanta. There are two Atlantas, the old and the new. Old Atlanta is staid; new Atlanta is modern and sophisticated. It's not a geographical division. Law offices next door to each other can have different styles. The skirted suit is good for new Atlanta. For old Atlanta, stick with the dress.

Boston. When you're in good old Boston, the home of the bean and the cod
Wear blue and gray for business, and brown for talking to God.
(No one else will listen.)

Chicago. Brown works as well here as blue and gray. Pantsuits test *very* negatively.

Dallas. Like Atlanta, this is a sophisticated Southern city. The skirted suit works very well here. For some reason, light green blouses and even light green dresses work well here in the summer.

Detroit. It's the only city in the country where brown works better than blue for a main garment.

Duluth. Women will do very well wearing dark green.

Houston. Outside of the large glass boxes downtown, Houston is a short-sleeve town. But businesswomen have to exude a lot of authority here. So I suggest dark colors, such as maroon and dark blue, for dresses.

Kansas City and St. Louis. Very, very persnickity places. You must look precise. Neatness counts everywhere, but in these cities there's an extraordinarily negative reaction to a woman whose hair is even slightly out of place or whose skirt is a little bit out of line.

Los Angeles. Although dresses work as well as skirted suits here, any dress that has a fun or play look is a strong negative.

Memphis. It's the only city in the United States where the dress tested better for businesswomen than the skirted suit.

Miami. The only city where the short-sleeved dress worked as well as the long-sleeved dress.

Milwaukee, Minneapolis, and St. Paul. You can get away with more green than you can in most other cities.

New Orleans. More than in any other city, red is acceptable for business.

New York. There are two New Yorks. On Wall Street, the successful businesswoman wears blue and gray skirted suits. But in the chic areas of New York, along Madison Avenue, a woman has to look somewhat fashionable.

Orlando. In spite of the relaxed atmosphere here, women must wear skirted suits. Light colors are best.

Philadelphia. Early in my career as a wardrobe engineer, I did some testing in Philadelphia. I came away baffled. Nothing seemed to quite mesh with the results I got in the rest of the country. I have since gotten used to Philadelphia's slightly maverick clothing reactions. General rules apply in

Philadelphia, but I learned that there are several "Philadelphia modifications."

Among those that apply to women: Orange works better than in most other places; with women, as with men, plaids can be a little more powerful; unlike in most cities, a solid black suit will give you a slightly higher credibility rating than a tweed suit (which is surprising in a city where horse-blanket plaid seems to pass muster).

I want to emphasize that the "Philadelphia phenomenon" is only slight. The differences are not major.

Pittsburgh. Some of the men can wear brown suits. Women should not.

Quebec. People in this city respond better to women in a high-fashion look than in any other city in North America. A businesswoman must never look dated. This means she must be at least six months ahead of New York. This also applies to French Canadian circles in Montreal.

San Antonio. Here, and in most of southern Texas, tan works as well as beige.

San Francisco. San Francisco is geographically in California and emotionally in the Northeast. It's a blue and gray town.

Seattle. A perfect test town. Nothing unusual happens. Blue, gray, and brown work equally well. Seattle is the typical Middle American city without being in the middle of America.

Washington, D. C. A Northeastern city that is not in the Northeast. Blue and gray only. No brown.

Chapter 4

Dressing for the Job

The research in this chapter is based on more than three thousand interviews with businesswomen, with their coworkers and superiors, and with top-ranking executives.

The sections on accountants, doctors, scientists, engineers, and secretaries are all based on several hundred interviews over the last five years. The job interview section is based on in-depth interviews with 412 men and women who were then hiring women. These men and women included personnel people who interview secretaries as well as corporate presidents seeking female executives. The research behind the sections on reporters and women in "glamour jobs" is described in those sections.

I could fill a book discussing my research on lawyers, since I've been researching lawyers for fifteen years. I spent countless hours in courtrooms and in interviews. Over the years, I have interviewed thousands of lawyers.

I hope this detailed analysis of the clothing requirements for success in several key careers will give women a better shot at the top.

HOW TO DRESS FOR JOB INTERVIEWS

When interviewing for a job, it is best to dress as if you were applying for a job one or two steps higher than the one for which you are interviewing.

If you are applying to be a secretary at a law firm and you dress like a lawyer instead of as a secretary, you will seem to be a bargain.

Obviously, your clothes can't suggest that you can't do the job; if you're applying to be an auto mechanic, you can't look as if you're scared of grease. So use common sense.

For any secretarial or clerical job, with the exception of those in the Deep South, the skirted suit is the best job-hunting outfit. (In the South a conservative dress works better.)

If you are applying for a secretarial or clerical job and you know the interviewer is a man, the best suit is light gray with a pale blue blouse. If the interviewer is a woman, the best suit is beige with a blue blouse. If you expect more than one interview on the same day, with both men and women interviewers, your best bet is a medium-range blue suit with a white blouse.

Every woman applying for a professional job should wear a skirted suit.

If you are applying for a professional, managerial, or executive job or any other job for which a college degree is required, the best-color suit in the North for most of the year is charcoal gray. In the Sun Belt and in the North in summer, the color is medium-range gray. Both outfits should be worn with a white blouse.

If you have a series of interviews for one job, you should definitely wear this suit for the most important interview. (Usually that is with the person who makes the final decision on whether to hire you.) If you are just graduating from college and can afford only one suit for job hunting, that is the outfit you should have.

If you are applying for any high-level job, you probably *will* go through several interviews. It's best to alternate your suits. If you know that on any particular day the only interview you will have will be a preliminary screening interview in the Personnel Department, a navy blue suit with a pale blue blouse (white if you are under five feet four inches) would be ideal. Another good suit for interviewing is light gray with a dark blue blouse.

At the executive level, you should carry an attaché case when you are interviewing. If you know you will be interviewed by a man, leave your handbag at home.

ACCOUNTANTS

The best uniform for women accountants is a solid gray suit with a white blouse. Second best is a charcoal gray suit with a white blouse, and third is a light gray suit with a white blouse. Quite obviously, the colors an accountant should be flying are gray and white.

Solid blue tests well too. Navy and medium-range blue suits with white blouses are the best of the blues.

Tweed does not test well on women accountants.

Women accountants should not carry handbags. They should carry a large, leather, masculine attaché case with a dial lock. The case should be at least four inches deep.

We found that when women accountants arrived in clients' offices dressed in conservative skirted suits, carrying the right attaché cases, and got right down to business with very little chitchat, they got a very high rating.

Impression is extremely important for accountants. Most clients have no way of knowing whether an accountant is effective or not. They're simply guessing at how good you are at accounting. So what you're selling is not expertise but the *impression* of your expertise.

And I'm afraid accounting is one area where drab does it.

REPORTERS

In doing the research for this section, I had help from some reporter friends. Six were from New York and 19 were from other cities. They reported to me on how people reacted to them when they wore specific outfits. These principles apply only to print reporters.

If you are a reporter, you do not want to intimidate your sources. If you do, they'll clam up. What you want to do is relax people and get them to talk.

So when you are dealing with the general public, you should avoid high-authority clothes. You can wear the skirted suit when you are interviewing business executives and powerful government officials, but a dark blue skirted suit with a contrasting blouse might threaten a clerk, a union leader, a bartender, a schoolteacher, a small-time politician or bureaucrat, or "the man on the street."

When dealing with such sources, your clothes can never say "I am better than you" or "I belong to a superior social class." Instead, your clothes should say "I'm one of you" or

"I'm not as important as one of you." That way people will like you, trust you, give you tips, and give you more detail. And all of that makes for better stories.

Whenever you cover any male-dominated group, such as the state legislature, the courthouse, or a men's sports team, you should not wear pants. Rural legislators, athletes, and others will not approve of the pants. Police have particularly strong expectations they want reporters to meet. They want to see male reporters in ties and women reporters in dresses.

If you are covering the White House, Congress, or any of the high-powered agencies in Washington, you will be dealing with upper middle class sources. You will connect with them in your power suit.

DOCTORS

Our tests on the proper clothes for women doctors were extensive. We had interns and residents at several large medical centers keep a record of patient and colleague reactions to them in various garments.

One result that surprised no one is that the white doctor jacket, with a prominently displayed stethoscope, and preferably with pen and pad also displayed, was the most effective authority garment for a young woman to wear. It announces to other staff members and to most patients that "this woman is a doctor," and she usually will be treated accordingly.

We had the women wear the white jacket with a variety of skirts, pants, and blouses. Our test results were as follows:

• The best skirts were wool or the look of wool, in a dark color and in a heavy material. They were knee-length or slightly lower.

• We found that in the South, linen or the look of linen in

slightly lighter colors worked just as well. In all sections of the country, polyester came in a poor third.

• Any skirt made of a material that had a high shine tested poorly.

• Skirt colors that tested best were dark blue, dark brown, black, and very dark maroon. Skirts that tested relatively well were medium-range blue, tan, beige, and very dark green.

• Skirt colors that tested poorly were all shades of the following: red, orange, yellow, pink, and lavender. Medium and light green tested especially poorly.

• Solid skirts tested best. Second best were traditional checks, plaids, and tweeds. All other patterns tested poorly.

I suggest that the woman doctor always wear a light-colored blouse. But not white. White blouses tend to make the jacket fall into itself and give the woman less presence and authority. The blouse should be man-tailored, or at least without ruffles, frills, or other feminine touches.

She should, whenever it's practical, stick with the white coat. When that's not possible, she should wear a skirted suit or a dress with a blazer or a skirt with a blazer.

The woman doctor should not wear a pendant. This is a very strong negative.

For accessories, the rules are almost the same as those for businesswomen—neutral-colored pantyhose, very simple handbag, and glasses that are neither large nor shaded. As little makeup as possible should be worn, and hair should be kept neat.

The one accessory that worked very well for businesswomen but poorly for female doctors was a leather case for carrying a pad. Many doctors in hospitals walk around with clipboards. The clipboard is an authority symbol for doctors, so it should be used.

At times the doctor acts as an executive. When she sits in a decision-making situation with colleagues or when she is put in charge of a department, she is, in every sense, an executive and must make an executive appearance.

LAWYERS

Although my first clients were law firms, I was in the clothes consulting business seven years before I was asked to advise a woman lawyer and another three years before I was hired to research the most effective dress for women lawyers in general. Since then I have counseled more than a hundred women lawyers, but it was a late and slow start. I hope this section of the book makes up for it.

The first assignment dealt not with the woman's role in the courtroom but in the boardroom. The advice I gave to that woman years ago remains valid today.

As a new partner in a prestigious firm, she was wearing two hats—counselor and executive. As an executive, her primary nonverbal message had to be "I am important" and "I am in charge." Skirted suits in traditional colors and cuts give off that message, so they were to be the backbone of her wardrobe.

She felt that such an austere look would not be appropriate for court appearances, and she wondered what to do on days she was scheduled for court. I advised her to keep a blue blazer and a beige blazer in her closet. When she came into the office, she was to don one whether it was a suitable aesthetic choice or not. Its function was to add instant nonverbal authority. She has been doing that for years with excellent results.

In the courtroom all lawyers are salespersons. The nonverbal messages they send are as important as the verbal ones. The rules for women lawyers, like the rules for saleswomen, are related to what they are selling and to whom they are selling it.

Dressing for the Judge

Since judges are a primary object of most presentations by lawyers, it is essential to dress to be credible with them.

Most judges are male and in their fifties. They spring from one of two clubs.

In small towns and rural areas, they come from country clubs. There is a good chance that their fathers were judges. They constitute sort of a local aristocracy.

Most of our research indicates that these judges take women lawyers lightly. It takes years to build credibility with these men, and in the beginning it is critical to appear professional in every way. So you should wear authority clothes. A skirted suit is the first choice. Next best is a dark blue dress. Never come across as a cute, frilly, or helpless female. It may seem like a convenient ploy to get by minor difficulties, but it will destroy your ability to be credible when it counts.

Most women working before judges, however, will be dealing with men who come out of political clubs. These big-city pols are far more accustomed to women lawyers than their small-town counterparts. They have worked their way up the social ladder and clawed their way through the political wars, so they are very sensitive about their authority and new social positions. Many have given up hefty incomes to become judges. The one rule with these men is never to pose a threat to them. Many of them would consider a woman in a slightly revealing dress a personal affront, and they would deal with her harshly. They will not announce publicly that they are ruling against you because your skirt is short, but—take my word for it—many of them will do it.

When addressing a judge without a jury, the socioeconomic style of your clothing is important. Both old-money and new-power judges are most apt to give credibility to a lawyer wearing upper middle class items. So any woman lawyer who comes from the lower class or lower middle class should learn to cross-shop.

The urban political clubs are producing a new type of judge, the outsider. These judges are black, Hispanic, and/or women.

This new breed of judge will give a woman lawyer her rights, and no more. They expect her to look and act like a professional. Any woman who plays cute or dresses cute before this type of judge will be making a serious mistake. Some of them look upon women lawyers as members of their club, and if they are women themselves, they will demand absolute professionalism. The ideal outfit for a woman appearing before these judges is the skirted suit.

Never forget the power of the judge, with or without a jury. Even as you observe all of the following advice on dressing for juries, you must obey the first rule of courtroom attire: If you think it will alienate the judge, don't wear it.

Dressing for the Jury

Dressing for a judge is easy compared to choosing your costume for juries. I realize that the juries you will deal with will never precisely fit the models I describe, but these models can serve you well as a general guide.

Old-money juries are almost extinct. If you do appear before one, be very conservative and upper middle class. Some grand juries also are homogenous. These juries are composed of successful men and women who think of themselves as the establishment. Many of them, through hard work and ability, have realized "the American dream." They tend to be well-off and look upon their life-style as a reward for virtue. Their first prejudice is the notion that people with money generally are more deserving than those without. Some sign of affluence is a positive with this jury.

Your best outfit before this group will depend on your approach. If you are going to argue from an authoritative position, a dark-colored skirted suit, blue or gray, would work well. But if you are going to use a friendly approach, a beige suit or dress would work better. Both outfits must be conservative, well tailored, and somewhat fashionable. The women on this jury will automatically relegate you to a lower status if your clothing looks cheap or dated.

Jurors who dress fashionably are particularly hard on women lawyers who do not. You must note carefully how women members of the jury are dressed. Take particular note if the foreman is a woman.

Most surburban juries are a mixture of income levels, but they are predominantly white. Treat a suburban jury with one or two minority members as if it were all white. Usually minority members who make it to suburbia are very solidly middle class.

I suggest simple conservative dresses with matching dress jackets or neutral contrasting blazers. Suits on women threaten any jurors with limited education. This, I hope, will change when women adopt the skirted suit as a uniform. If this type of juror becomes conditioned to expect women in suits, women lawyers will fare much better.

I know of one lawyer who wears dresses when working with this type of jury, except when she believes that the case will rest on her authority. Then she switches to conservative suits for summations.

If you are going to wear a suit, make it dark blue with a white blouse. This is the color combination that men and women in the lower socioeconomic suburban group associate with important occasions and important people. Whatever you do, avoid charcoal gray suits, since they—along with

117

all other status symbols, such as designer scarves and bags, mink coats, and expensive-looking jewelry—will destroy your credibility with this group.

If the jury is in blue-collar suburbia, treat it the same as the mixed socioeconomic bag.

If the jury is made up largely of executives, professionals, and other comfortable suburbanites, the rules change dramatically. Your best outfit is a charcoal gray suit with a pale blue cotton blouse. You should also wear one good piece of jewelry, carry a good leather attaché case, and take your notes with the appropriate gold pen.

Any look that could be considered chic by your most backward friend will kill you before a rural jury. They don't like urban shakers and movers. Male lawyers have an advantage with this jury because they can loosen their ties and roll up their sleeves. Your best approach is a simple dress with a high neckline and long sleeves combined with a low-key approach.

Urban juries are so varied that the rules change with each jury.

If the urban jury is predominantly white and upper middle class, you should dress in almost the same style as before a suburban upper middle class white jury, with one major difference. Upper middle class city women are far more fashionable and up to date than suburbanites. You must look as if you could be a member of their group.

Fashion for the woman lawyer is a time bomb. If she looks dated to women or chic to men, she will lose credibility. Proceed carefully.

Urban ghetto blacks on a jury tilt things in your favor. Most of these blacks have a strong antiestablishment attitude, and they do not necessarily consider women part of the establishment. You must avoid anything in your attire that says establishment. Under no circumstance wear a suit or even a very conservative dress. A dress that is somewhat colorful without being gaudy will work best. The colors that tested best are beige, lavender, maroon, deep green, blue, and yellow.

Black Lawyers

None of the above advice applies to black women lawyers. They should wear conservative blue, gray, brown, and beige suits only. With the appropriate conservative blouse, this gives off a positive message to all segments of society. To her fellow blacks she is announcing that she has made it in a white man's world. To white jurors she announces that by dressing conservatively she is going along. The only time a black woman lawyer might consider bending this rule is when she is working with an urban black ghetto jury. Here she might wear items that would be identifiable as black, particularly if her opponent is also black.

Dressing Your Client to Win

Lawyers want to control the communications between their client and the judge or jury. Naturally this should include nonverbal communication.

If you want the judge and jury to believe that your client is innocent, the client should *look* innocent. Youth and innocence are synonymous in the minds of most people. If you can make your client look young, you are halfway home. Clean hair helps and facial hair hurts. Beards and mustaches cut into your client's credibility and destroy any look of innocence.

If your client is a male, a blue suit, white shirt, and solid maroon tie say innocent. If your client is a female, a conservative navy blue dress with a white accent says innocent. A man's hair should be relatively short, while the ideal length for a woman's hair is shoulder length. Anything that adds to the well-scrubbed, churchgoer look will give you an advantage. The look of innocence cuts across all racial, economic, and sexual lines.

It is especially important that you orchestrate your client's clothing when he or she is testifying. When you have a man under direct questioning, put him in a soft gray or medium-blue suit, depending on the socioeconomic level of the jury. Add a white or pale blue shirt and a blue or maroon tie with a simple pattern.

If your client is a woman, she could wear a solid blue or beige dress with a simple piece of jewelry.

Both of the looks are highly credible and somewhat authoritative without being offensive. And those looks are easy to look at. Research indicates that an audience will remember and believe more of what a man says when they can look at him without straining.

When your client or witness is under cross-examination, you can let his clothing do the opposite, make the jurors forget—unless you specifically want them to remember. A plaid suit with a shirt that clashes in color and line and a very bright tie, or a dress with an impossible pattern to look at (such as a series of diminishing circles) will work without offending and can cut in half the effect of a strong cross-examination.

One other device is to have your client wear glasses during cross-examination. One lawyer had his client's windowpane glasses treated so they gave off an unpleasant glare. Nobody on the jury looked directly at him for two days.

There are other messages that clothing can send in a courtroom. If your client is injured, he or she is more likely to be believed if the clothing is slightly too large.

If a man's clothing is too large, it will be harder for many people to believe that he is guilty of the misuse of power.

You can drive home your client's impotent image by dressing him in soft colors: pale blue and beige. For a woman, the best colors are pale blue, pink, or yellow.

If your client is accused in a conspiracy, both you and he should disassociate yourselves from the other defendants and their lawyers. Looking different here could be more important than looking honest or authoritative.

SCIENTISTS AND ENGINEERS

If you are a laboratory scientist and if it is standard procedure in your lab to wear a coat or a smock, you should wear one. Under it you should wear a solid-colored dark skirt and a light-colored blouse. But the blouse should not be the same color as the smock. A white blouse works well with a light blue smock. A light blue blouse is a good choice with a white smock.

You should also wear skin-colored pantyhose and traditional pumps with about an inch-and-a-half heel.

If a smock or jacket is optional, you should pass on the option as often as possible, unless you are in an office where only the scientists wear the smock and it is a status symbol. If you are in an office where everybody wears a smock, I would suggest that whenever possible you slip into a jacket that matches your skirt and that you wear the businesswoman's outfit described in the earlier sections of this book. Under no circumstances should women in this position wear a vest with the suit.

Women in scientific laboratory jobs may also wear dresses. However, dresses should always be solid, pinstriped, or paisley, never floral and never in any of the colors, such as pink or lavender, which have traditionally been considered feminine.

Your dresses should always be a strong contrasting color with the smock or the jacket, and the dress should always be knee length or slightly below.

You must be very careful not to clash in color or in line. Scientists tend to come from lower middle class backgrounds, and they are conservative in their judgment of clothing. They will respect you a lot more if your clothing is simple in pattern and color and is very carefully coordinated. At the same time, you must be equally careful not to look too well put together. A look of precision on the scientist somehow turns off other scientists.

The look of high fashion is deadly in the laboratory. If you have the figure to wear models' clothes, don't wear them in the lab. You will be considered a lightweight and less of a scientist than your sister scientists who wear conservative clothing. The same applies to women who are engineers.

We took pictures of the same woman and showed them to one hundred engineers. In the first picture the woman was dressed like a fashion model. In the second picture she wore the standard businesswoman's attire. We asked each of the engineers to judge the woman's ability as an engineer. There were 88 male engineers and 12 female engineers. Ninety-four of the engineers chose the woman in the standard business garb as the more competent, more reliable, and better engineer. Six engineers chose the woman who looked like a fashion model. Five of the 6 who chose the high-fashion woman were women themselves. Only one man chose the high-fashion look as being the look of competence.

The results of that project are particularly important for those scientists and engineers who do not work closely with the people who make the decisions about their promotions. If the chief engineer or chief of the laboratory looks out and sees you staring into space, he will either assume that you're thinking or that you're daydreaming. If he has been preconditioned as most of us have, the conservative look will say "thinking," and the high-fashion look will say "daydreaming."

We have visited over a hundred laboratories. In them we found only two women in charge, even though one-fourth of the employees in all of those labs were women. Both of those women bosses dressed exactly as I recommend. And both made the same comment—there is so much male chauvinism in science that, in order to succeed, a woman needs to be extremely effective in every way, including her dress.

WOMEN IN GLAMOUR INDUSTRIES

The so-called glamour jobs tend to be in high-fashion industries. Such industries recruit some highly talented young women. These women move rapidly into positions of power; then they plateau. The women who are producers of major television shows and editors or assistant editors at major publishing houses tend to earn less money and get fewer promotions than men in comparable positions.

I suspect that sexism might be one reason. But another reason is totally the fault of the women themselves. Many of them dress for failure.

The standard look is casual chic: lots of denim and corduroy. Boots are popular.

When I started making guest appearances on TV shows, my first impression of the young women producers was that they were good-looking assistants. When I found out that they really planned the shows and wielded a lot of power, I was amazed.

For this book I did a survey of 162 businessmen, all of whom had been on one or more TV shows. I asked them to guess at the salary, educational level, and authority of the women who produce the shows.

The average of the salary guesses was $12,000 a year. Many of these women make a lot more than that.

The average guess on educational background was two years of college. Virtually all of these women are college graduates.

The men also guessed that the women had no real power. Wrong again.

The message these women were giving off was that they were not in charge of anything and that they were there to speak for someone else.

The top executives of CBS, NBC, ABC, and most publishing houses dress in the same manner as the executives of General Motors, IBM, and U.S. Steel. A woman who aspires to join such an executive club—and it is a club—should wear a dark skirted suit that says, "I am a career-minded woman who is going to make it to the top in this business."

HOW TO AVOID STAYING A SECRETARY

If you are a secretary or a general clerical worker, don't dress like one unless you have no further ambitions. Secretaries, particularly in small companies or in small departments of large companies, often function as executive assistants. More than one man in top management owes his success to his secretary's executive ability, not his own. That is why many men take their secretaries with them when they switch jobs or even companies. Yet very few secretaries get the title or the pay of an executive assistant, and fewer become executives in their own right.

One reason is that they usually announce—unintentionally, with their clothing—that they are satisfied with their position.

In one survey of 34 secretaries, we found 18 who definitely wanted to move up. Nine of them believed that they had a realistic shot at a better position. When we surveyed their bosses, however, only 2 believed that their secretary wanted to do anything else.

When we told one of the women what her boss said, she claimed that her boss had to be deaf and blind. We pointed out that he might be deaf, but he certainly was not blind, for he had read her nonverbal message. She was wearing an inexpensive polyester pantsuit and had a sweater hung around her shoulders and tied by the sleeves. She admitted that neither of those things was ever done by any of the women who held the position she aspired to.

The rule for all businesswomen is to *dress for the job you want, not the job you have.* Polyester pantsuits, sweaters, slacks, skirt and blouse outfits, and dresses with large prints all announce that you have no ambition.

The skirted suit must become the mainstay of any woman who aspires to an executive position. It announces that you think of yourself as a candidate for bigger and better things. Unless you believe you are ready to move up, no one else will.

Chapter 5

Selling Yourself and Other Important Items

True equality of the sexes will have arrived in corporate America when at least half of the vice-presidents for sales are women. The sales vice-presidency is a good yardstick for measuring women's success because sales is the lifeblood of the American business system. The only way women will get those vice-presidencies is, of course, by being crackerjack saleswomen.

But it isn't only the women who want to be vice-presidents in charge of sales who should be concerned about their sales ability.

The ability to sell is critical to all women who wish to

move in any branch of corporate, social, or political America. Your ability to sell products, ideas, concepts, and yourself to others will play a vital role in determining your success. Therefore, this chapter must be read carefully by all women who want to make an impact on their environment.

Theoretically, women should dominate the sales field. From early youth they surpass males in two of the most important skills required for sales: the ability to "read" people and verbal communications. Yet in sales roles, where those two critical skills are always operating, they often fail.

Research has proven conclusively that the clothing a salesperson wears will affect his or her chances of making a sale. Further, research by a series of experts has established that when a person gives off contradictory verbal and nonverbal messages, the nonverbal message is the one more likely to be believed.

My research indicates that most women, most of the time, give off nonverbal messages that would be negative in a sales situation. And this is the primary reason for their failure.

We have researched the effect of clothing with respect to several factors in sales situations, including

The appearance of the buyer

The age of the seller
The age of the buyer

The socioeconomic level of the seller
The socioeconomic level of the buyer

The race of the seller
The race of the buyer

The geographical base of the seller
The geographical base of the buyer

The training and industrial specialty of the buyer

The sex of the seller
The sex of the buyer

The product

THE NO-SALE LOOK

I should point out that I virtually guarantee my corporate clients that I will improve the performance of their sales forces. It is on this basis that I charge substantial fees to the largest corporations in America, Europe, and the Orient. Unless I did exactly what I said I was going to do, they would not continue to engage me year in and year out.

To even be considered by these highly prestigious firms, I had to prove to them, before tampering with their sales forces, that it was necessary to do something. So we ran a series of experiments. In these tests, we used saleswomen extensively.

In one test, we gave purchasing agents two buttons, one positive and one negative. We told them to push the appropriate button as soon as they received a positive or negative message. (The result was recorded, but the saleswomen were not aware of the buttons.) In 94 percent of the cases when they pressed the negative button, they did so before the saleswoman had said one word.

In most of the cases where the negative button was pressed, not only did the saleswoman fail to make the sale, but very little communication took place. The purchasing agent either kept working while the saleswoman was there, set up impossible specifications, or complained about price when it really wasn't an issue. A couple of the agents even made passes. The purchasing agents did just about everything except give the saleswomen an opportunity to sell a product.

On two occasions the purchasing agent dismissed the saleswoman and then had to call her company and have her return. In both cases the product was only available through that company, and the purchasing agent needed it desperately and immediately. But he was so overwhelmed by the negative nonverbal impression he had of the saleswoman that he dismissed her.

That strong negative reaction to immediate nonverbal messages is not sexist; similar experiments with men yielded almost identical results.

Most of these saleswomen had not met the purchasing agents before this test meeting. However, in postpresentation interviews, the saleswomen indicated that from their previous experience they could have accurately guessed the agents' general appearance and socioeconomic levels. Most of the saleswomen did not take those factors into consideration when choosing their clothing for the meeting. But they should have.

SELLING TO THREE TYPES OF MEN

If the buyer is a man, his general appearance will fall into one of three categories:

1. Executive type, with an authoritative suit and tie.
2. Nonexecutive suit-and-tie type. (His clothes will be lower middle class or some other form that indicates that he is not headed for the executive ranks.)
3. Nonsuit and tie type.

When dealing with executives, a saleswoman generally will perform best when she is dressed in appropriate executive attire. The skirted suit with contrasting blouse works best. If she feels that she must add authority to her presentation, she can keep her glasses on (if she wears glasses). She

129

may also wear a hat in an office providing it is brimmed and not particularly masculine. Naturally, she should carry all the other appropriate executive accessories.

When selling to the nonexecutive type, the saleswoman should realize that she is dealing with a conformist, but one who may be threatened by a very high authority suit. She should wear a traditional conservative dress, and she will be far safer if her accessories don't pack so much power. A simple black attaché case would probably work better with this man than the expensive brown leather one that you would carry when selling to a top executive. Never wear a hat in this man's presence, since high-authority items on women might appear to be a threat to his manhood. And if you pose such a threat, it will be "No Sale" time.

With the nonsuited or blue-collar man, you have a variety of choices.

Surprisingly, this man will often react well to the woman who wears a high-power suit—particularly if he is in a macho field, such as construction or the heavy equipment business, which doesn't require that he wear a suit and tie. But as a general rule, we would suggest that you wear a conservative dress with this man also, unless you know that he is a power figure in his own area. The only absolute negative rule with him is never wear anything that even resembles the look of a fashion model. If you look chic in any way, he will think you're a dilettante, not a salesperson. And he'll send you packing.

WHAT MAKES OLDER MEN BUY?

Since women have only recently moved into sales in any numbers, they generally will be younger than the people they're selling to. So it is essential that they learn how to dress to sell to older men.

Another man will have an advantage when selling to a man; he can build a relationship with him of comradeship. At first our research could find no comparative advantage for women. When women attempted to become friendly with the purchasing agents, there were almost always sexual overtones, and this hurt their ability to sell.

But we did uncover one way for women to cut into all that fraternity and fellowship.

In research we had conducted earlier for fund-raisers, we discovered a very interesting phenomenon. When one man was raising money from another, the decision was often strictly an emotional one. Obviously, if a man was raising money for a conservative cause, he went to a man who had a reputation for giving money to such causes. The man he went to was often rich and gave away X number of dollars a year, depending on the advice his accountant gave him. Whom he gave the money to was purely a matter of personal preference. We discovered that a fund-raiser wearing symbols of this man's youth was far more likely to be successful than one who was not.

One fund-raiser who was dealing with a fifty-seven-year-old man looked up the Brooks Brothers ties that were popular when the man was in high school and college. Those ties were the early Ivy League look, with deep-colored stripes. He discovered that some of those ties were still around.

For another client he came up with a hand-painted tie. In both cases he pulled down a lot of money.

This is one of the few occasions where the research on men's clothing was a tremendous help to the research on women's clothing. We discovered that a woman could more than offset the male-to-male advantage if she wore or included in her ensemble elements of style that were part of the purchaser's youth.

If she knew or could guess the man's exact age, she could go through old magazines at the library and discover what was being worn by young girls when he was sixteen, seventeen, and eighteen. If she included in her ensemble an element of that look, we found that she substantially increased her chances of making the sale.

For a man forty, a pleated skirt may well remind him of his youth in the early 1950s. However, the skirt cannot have a kick pleat or look dated in any other way. And, of course, this principle shouldn't be carried to extremes. Don't show up in bobby socks, saddle shoes, and a poodle skirt.

I cannot emphasize too much the importance of this finding. We increased the sales of 18 out of 20 women in a Midwestern group of saleswomen by 5 percent or more. At the same time the sales of the men in the same corporate group and the industry overall slipped by 3 percent.

As potent a weapon as this is with older men, it will not work with men who are younger than the saleswoman or about the same age. Furthermore, when a woman wears clothes that are chic, "in," or with-it—clothes that are attractive to a man her own age or younger—the implications are immediately sexual. And she will lose her authority. It is a very delicate line, and women must walk it with a great deal of care.

ADJUSTING YOUR CLOTHES TO THE BUYER'S LEVEL

You have to adjust your look to the buyer's socioeconomic background or level. Here you have to feel your way around some. If the buyer is someone you deal with regularly, try to figure out which predominates: his background or his level.

Many men from a lower middle class background never shed the traces of that background, while others graduate to upper middle class style. Estimate where your buyer (male or female) is on that scale and dress in the same manner.

If the buyer is lower middle and you are upper middle, don't follow your natural dressing instincts. If most of your buyers are lower middle and you are upper middle, you will have to spend as much time cross-shopping to learn how to dress down as someone who is lower middle will to dress up. Obviously, you should never wear high-fashion clothing when dealing with a lower middle class buyer.

If the situation is reversed—you come from a lower socioeconomic background and you're dealing with an upper middle class buyer—you should be extremely careful not to wear lower middle class clothing. Such clothing wouldn't offend your buyer, but it would cut your authority and your credibility. People at upper social levels tend to believe and trust only people who have and wear the status symbols of their group.

SELLING TO BLACKS

The greatest difficulty that most white middle class salesmen have is selling to blacks. That difficulty is not shared by most white women. They have a higher credibility with blacks than white men do, providing they don't wear very dark authoritative colors or anything that makes them look dated. The average black regards the look and feel of the 1950s as a throwback to a time when blacks did not fare well. And they feel that people who support these looks will also support the same ideas that held blacks back.

The general rule for selling to blacks is always dress up to date and with it, without ever being too chic.

BLACK SALESWOMEN

Black saleswomen are in an extremely good position from one standpoint and an extremely poor one from another.

They make a first impression that is not likely to offend anyone. Almost all elements in our society will welcome a black woman's sales presentation without prejudging her.

However, black women dealing with middle-class white executives have an authority problem. It is unfortunate, but the preconditioning of the white male executive in particular has led him to believe that black women are lower middle class or lower class. They react negatively to a black woman who takes an authority position—unless she arms herself with all obvious props of authority.

Therefore, all the rules for white saleswomen are thrown out the window for blacks. I suggest that all black saleswomen wear as many high authority and status items as they can. The expensive pen, the right attaché case, and the beautiful wool suit are not simply decorations—they are essential to the black saleswoman.

When a black woman dresses right, she is probably the most exceptional salesperson there is.

SALES AND GEOGRAPHY

Geography is a big, big factor. And saleswomen must understand its nuances. Saleswomen think the same outfit will carry the day anywhere in the country. It won't. What plays in Peoria can fail in Philadelphia.

The Northeast

The most conservative business area in the United States is the Washington–New York–Boston corridor. Most corporate headquarters have the feel of the conservative Northeast, although some that have been in the South and the Southwest for years are beginning to lose it. However, I advise any woman who is selling in corporate headquarters to show up in her most conservative, northeastern-establishment garments.

The men she meets in the conservative areas and at corporate headquarters will generally be wearing dark and medium-range gray suits and dark and medium-range blue suits with or without pinstripes. They avoid brown and the saleswoman should too. She should dress in the same vein as the men. But she should avoid the pinstriped suit because it never works for a woman. If she wears a scarf when dealing with these people, they will respond positively to the patterns they are used to seeing on their male colleagues—polka dots, paisleys, simple stripes, solids, plaids, and foulards, which say "Daddy went to Yale" in men's ties and "I am a member of the club" in women's scarves.

When a Northeasterner is selling in another part of the country, she should avoid the Ivy League patterns. Solid scarves and less sophisticated patterns will work much better. If your instinct tells you that the company or area you're dealing with is not heavily conservative, you might try plaid or tweed in skirted suits.

One very successful saleswoman does a lot of worthwhile "casing" of a new company. When she has an appointment at a company with which she has never dealt before, she makes the appointment for either very early in the morning or just after lunch. This gives her a chance to take a look at the employees walking in and out of the company. It gives her a feel for the general dress code of the company, and it tells her a great deal about the expectations of the people she is about to meet. She carries in her car several scarves, two attaché cases, and a few other minor changes, and she adapts her wardrobe to suit the message the company gives her. She is one of America's most successful salespersons, making more than $100,000 a year.

There are general guidelines for certain areas of the country. But remember that they are not ironclad. You must analyze each company.

The South

In the South women tend to be more traditionally dressed. If you're selling in the South, you are probably better off wearing a dress.

If you are a non-Southern woman selling in the South, you are working under two disadvantages: (1) You're working in an area where women have not made the greatest strides and (2) you are an outsider. Southerners give greater credibility to other Southerners than they do to outsiders. This is why corporations tend to hire Southerners to sell in the South.

You should avoid any overly sophisticated look that identifies you as an outsider. There are only two highly sophisticated cities in the South: Atlanta and Dallas. In these cities you might wear the same outfit you could wear in New York or Los Angeles. In the rest of the South, you must be quite a bit more traditional.

There are important don'ts in the South. Here are some of them:

• Don't ever wear a brimmed hat into a man's office.
• Don't wear any item that is identifiable as masculine.
• Never wear a vest. It is a death knell for any saleswoman.
• Never wear lavender or any shade of purple.
• Never wear a black dress or suit.
• If you are invited to a business lunch, don't drink. Sixty-two percent of Southern men think it is unwise for a woman to drink while doing business.

The formality level in the South varies from city to city and from industry to industry. There are entire industries in the South that are short-sleeve industries, and both men and women dress informally. You must not make the mistake of becoming that informal, partly because Southerners are not yet as accustomed to thinking of women as executives. Therefore, you must never wear anything that could say "I am a secretary" or "I am at leisure."

The one image a saleswoman must project in the South is total professionalism. You must always wear a suit. Naturally the suit can be made of cotton, but I would suggest a cotton and polyester mix. Even though that is not as comfortable, it will look better at the end of the day.

Lighter colors are worn in the South. If you choose a blue suit, it should be a medium-range blue. A gray suit should be a lot lighter than charcoal. And you may wear suits in brighter, lighter colors. However, if you wear pink, lavender, pale yellow, or very light gold, you will immediately destroy your authority. In the South these and other very traditional feminine colors are associated with the woman who is anything but an executive.

If you are a Southern woman in the South, there is an entirely different set of rules. For years Southern women have been powerful figures in ruffles. Southerners are accustomed to powerful women—the Scarlett O'Hara breed. I know several Southern women who dress in very frilly Southern feminine gear and outsell most men in the office. You can get away with this only if you are a Southerner and over thirty-five. If you are under thirty-five, you should lean toward conservatism.

Some Southern businesswomen try to take that very effective Southern-belle image North or West. And it falls flat. Any woman dressed in the very feminine colors and patterns that work well on some women in the South is categorized as a loser in most Northern areas. When you leave the South, leave the patterns and colors of the South behind. Everything you wear should be three shades darker and two degrees more conservative.

Southern women also must avoid wearing Mexican or cowboy items worn by some businessmen in the Southwest. A businessman can get away with the Texas hat in San Antonio; he can get away with the Mexican jewelry in New Mexico. But a businesswoman cannot.

The Midwest

Theory holds that the Midwest is conservative clothing country. But theory is not fact. Businesswear in the Midwest is brighter than in the Northeast and less traditional than in the South. A woman in the Midwest can actually operate in some areas rather successfully wearing a pantsuit. I'm *not* suggesting it. I'm pointing it out only to illustrate that all the stories about the Midwest being the citadel of conservatism are exaggerated. It is conservative, but it isn't the conservative capital of the Western world.

A woman in the Northeast can sometimes get away with wearing a dress, but women in the Midwest have not yet established the corporate clout they have along the Eastern seaboard. Therefore, it is more difficult for a woman in the Midwest to operate successfully as an executive, and she must prove her authority every minute of the day. It is my advice that any woman selling in this area wear only skirted suits—only in traditional colors and only in traditional patterns—unless, of course, her product or some other factor dictates otherwise. Blue, gray, and brown work equally well in most of the Midwest.

Midwesterners recoil from people who wear items that remind them of the Eastern establishment. This represents a major problem for women. As I pointed out, the best garment for woman to wear is generally the skirted suit. But to some Midwesterners the skirted suit represents the pushy Eastern woman. Don't give up your suit; it will help you much more than it will hurt you. But when you are going to be dealing with someone who might have a negative reaction to a high-authority suit, you can shift to a suit in a softer color.

The golden rule for anybody selling in the Midwest is that you must look rich and successful to sell. For men, this means big cars. For women, it means equally expensive but smaller cars. Sports cars work well. A huge car reduces a woman's authority.

Wear only the best of everything—expensive suits, good jewelry. Try not to pay less than $100 for an attaché case. Even if it weren't tasteful, it would work better than a cheaper case.

Southern California

When I talk to corporate groups, I often say that I will have to make exceptions to everything I've said for people who come from such foreign countries as Britain, France, and Southern California. Southern California is the only section of the country where informality works better than formality. And that is tough on businesswomen. It is extremely difficult for them to establish authority in the leisurely clothing of Southern California.

Our research does not prove much. Sometimes wearing very traditional conservative clothing worked best, and sometimes wearing leisure clothing worked best. This is the only area of the country where we cannot guarantee the skirted suit to be more efficient than the pantsuit or the dress. We can guarantee that it is more efficient than a skirt and blouse or slacks and a blouse. The only advice I have for women selling in Southern California is to play it by ear and if you are going to sin, sin on the side of being conservative.

DRESSING FOR YOUR PRODUCT

A saleswoman must dress to match her product. This means she must look as if she is able to use it well. For a woman selling almost any business-oriented product, this would mean the standard skirted suit. But for a woman selling fashion, it would mean the latest look.

Looking as if you know how to use your product does not necessarily mean that you look as if you are about to use it at that very moment. For example, a woman who sells tennis equipment obviously need not wear a tennis dress.

139

The best example of dressing to suit a product that I ever saw was a woman who sold high-risk securities in Florida. When she sold them at the watering stops of the rich and retired, she looked as if she were on constant vacation. She knew that they were buying comfortable leisure. But when she sold downtown, she dressed in a conservative two-piece gray suit that was two shades darker than the grays the local stores were selling. She said that people in the downtown offices liked the possible high return, but they also liked to feel that they were buying a secure investment. Her choice of dark gray successfully gave them a sense of security.

SELLING TO WOMEN

There is a small bagful of tricks you can use to get across to other women the message that you are important.

Most women feel that certain elements of fashion are an essential ingredient for being well dressed. Therefore, if you are dealing only with women, your outfit should include something that would be considered high fashion. For example, in the early 1970s when the fashion industry was pushing hardest on the midi, a midi-length skirted suit would have been the ideal uniform for a woman in charge of other women.

Another way to hint that you're in touch with fashion is to wear this year's color. This is the best route to take if you have both men and women working for you. A blouse in the right color can be authoritative and chic at the same time. But if the "in" color turns out to be purple, green, or gold, don't wear it. Any positive fashion impact would be offset by people's negative reactions to those colors.

Male executives will think less of you for wearing designer scarves or carrying designer handbags, but women will not. And one-third of the women will give you a higher status rating if you have these items.

The most important thing to remember when dealing with other women is that women expect precision. Everything must be just so. When your blouse picks up the color of the accent thread in your tweed suit, it must pick it up exactly. A near miss won't make it. Your hair must always be exactly in place. Your desk and general surroundings should be immaculate and orderly enough to pass a military inspection.

We found that the skirted suit works as well with other women as the pantsuit, but no better. So the following information can be applied to either ensemble: Navy blue suits with white or beige blouses will definitely communicate your importance to other women. So will a solid gray or charcoal gray suit with a white blouse. Tweed suits will work, too, partly because tweed is now fashionable.

BUSINESS AND INDUSTRIAL SALES

Research shows that major purchases of business and industrial equipment are usually made on the authority of the salesperson, not on the expertise of the purchaser.

Naturally your authority is greater if you work for a major corporation. If you sell for IBM, General Motors, or any other giant, your clothing should help you capitalize on the reputation of the company. If your company is a heavyweight, you should be a heavyweight. Everything you say, do, and wear should emphasize that you are an important person from that very important corporation. Even though you are a salesperson and not an executive, you should come off as an executive when you are selling to executives. That way you will piggyback the credentials of your firm, and your sale will be that much easier. Power might corrupt, but it also sells.

Wear dark skirted suits and rich, conservative blouses that contrast sharply with your suit. Your shoes should be plain pumps. To maintain your power image, you should not wear light-colored suits for important appointments, even in the summer, although light materials are all right.

If you are working for a small, unheralded company that's competing with giants, your task is more difficult. You're not coming in with Big Name Corp behind you.

The saleswoman for a giant is measured against the buyer's image of the corporation. But when you represent the Dingdong Computer Co. or the One Wrench Motor Co., you probably have to stake out your corporate image. Your company is judged largely by the image you project.

If a saleswoman for IBM or General Motors shows up in atrocious clothing, the buyer will simply say she is a dummy working for IBM or General Motors. However, if that dummy works for a little-known company, the buyer will assume it's a third-rate company. You have to project for your company an image of weight and power, as well as competence and reliability.

For that reason, you should follow the same dress code I spelled out for the representative of a giant corporation.

Stock up on skirted suits with high-contrast blouses. Adorn yourself with all the executive trimmings. You don't have as much margin as the saleswoman for a giant corporation. She can afford to miss the mark now and then. But you must be on target every day because you must sell yourself and your company before you can sell your product.

Selling Smaller Items

Women who sell relatively minor office equipment— office supplies, business forms, and so on—are working in an entirely different market and with a different set of rules. The people who buy from them are not major executives. They might be overwhelmed by the dark skirted suit, hat, and good attaché case. You can stick with skirted suits, but you should wear slightly softer colors. Medium-range blue or beige will do. You can carry a good handbag and wear good shoes, but don't stagger people with massive doses of affluence.

These people are not headed for executive positions, and many of them will be jealous of people who look like they're going to make it. If they're in the driver's seat when they're dealing with a fast-track junior executive, they're going to do their best to slow her down. I would suggest items that say, "I'm not on the way up." Your clothes should say, "I'm clean and reliable," and no more.

Selling in a Profit Sequence

When you are selling in a profit sequence, you're not selling carpeting to John Molloy for his living room. You're selling it to a store, which will make money selling it to Molloy.

In any profit sequence, you are not selling carpeting or cars or typewriters or anything else—except profit. You are, in effect, asking another businessperson to go into business with you, and that person only wants to go into business with somebody who is successful. You, therefore, must reek of success.

Your clothes need not be conservative—that depends on your product. But you must dress richly. And you should drive a good car, preferably one that screams wealth—a sports car or a Mercedes is ideal.

Carry only the finest attaché case; wield only gold pens. You might even want to wear large, obvious jewelry.

This is one case where you not only should but *must* look more prosperous than the people you are selling to. You have to make them think they'll ride high on your prosperity. That's particularly true if you're dealing with people who have limited funds.

These principles are operating when you're dealing with a

Ma and Pa carpet store and when you're selling to the largest carpet distributor in the world.

SELLING YOUR EXPERTISE

I know an artist who is a nonpareil at dressing to look like an expert. As a result, she's an expert at selling her paintings. I met her when we were testing artists in New York.

Whenever she was painting, she looked like a housewife. But when she went to sell or to baby-sit her paintings at gallery shows, she went into character and put on her "artist's clothing."

Her outfits were colorful, kooky, and exotic. Everyone referred to her as "that way-out artist over in the corner." In that garb she sells her paintings for thousands of dollars, and she is convinced that she wouldn't have such big paydays if she tried to sell while wearing her mufti.

She told me her costume was itself a painting. She said that in putting together her ensemble, she was simply creating the impressions people expected. But the evolution of her marketing system was far from a casual decision to wear freaky clothes.

For three years she took notes on what she was wearing every time a stranger asked her if she were an artist. After studying her notes, she decided that certain colors, patterns, and cuts of clothing made people think she was artistic. And she used those colors, cuts, and patterns as the basis for her sales costumes.

Anybody can adopt a variation of her research. At the end of every sales sequence, you can write down exactly what you were wearing and what type of reaction you received. After you have done this for several months, patterns will emerge. You will discover that certain garments work better than others. That will help you make your clothes work for you.

If your expertise is in an area that has traditionally been masculine, you will have to bend over backward to convince people that you're really an expert.

We stationed a young woman in a garage and then sent people in with their ailing cars. She was supposed to diagnose the problem and tell the customers what had to be done. Most of them reacted rather negatively when she was dressed in anything feminine or frilly. The minute she put on coveralls, her credibility shot up. When she put some grease on her hands and face, it increased even more. When she looked as if she was working on the cars, her credibility increased a third time.

What all of this means is that in certain areas the look of expertise is definitely unfeminine.

SELLING REAL ESTATE

Women dominate real estate sales. One reason is that they're good at it.

This is one area where women seem to know how to dress for their job. We tested the outfits women wear when selling property and found that the best saleswomen knew what they were doing. They dressed to match the property they were selling. When they were selling country property, they looked as if they might be living on a country place of their own. Tweed dresses and little country hats worked well. When they were selling expensive suburban houses, they dressed stylishly, and when they were selling commercial property, they donned skirted suits and blouses. Dressing to match the property is the most important commandment, whether you're trying to sell the property or trying to convince a seller to list with you.

Here are a few more hints.

- Dress as if you were going to be the ideal neighbor.
- Always wear the colors or patterns that will let your

buyer trust you. If the buyer comes from a lower middle class background, the ideal colors are blue with white accent, deep brown with a very light beige accent, or a combination of deep maroon and navy blue.

If, however, you're dealing with upper middle class people, the classic blue and beige combinations with a slightly better handbag and a slightly nicer pair of shoes will work. So will a gray blazer over a dress or a gray dress by itself.

• Unlike most businesswomen, you must drive a big car, but it should not be an overly expensive one. The car that elicits the most trust from other women is a station wagon. It says, "I'm a housewife like you. I'm not a hustler or one of those big-city slickers who is going to take you."

• Your car must be immaculate. A messy car can kill your sale because women have little respect for women with messy cars.

• If you are going to show property that is difficult to walk on, you must wear shoes that will take you through snow or mud without looking as if it's an effort. If you look as if the mud or snow is about to stop you, it could stop your sales momentum.

• Never wear expensive or gaudy jewelry.

• The less lipstick and other makeup you wear, the better.

• If you take people back to the office, sit out front with them. Don't sit behind the desk and have them sit out front.

Probably the most important thing to remember is that when people buy a house, they do not buy bricks, mortar, and timber. They buy a feeling of community. If you're the only contact they have with that community, they will judge it by your clothes, your habits, and your speech patterns. They will reject you, the community, and the house if they don't like what they see and hear.

Chapter 6

Dressing to Attract Men

When I was sixteen, the Charles Atlas ads discouraged me. They always told of how the skinny fellow built up a pile of muscles and got the girl. It looked grim for me because I looked like Mr. Before. By the time I discovered that women liked thin men and not big muscles, I had gained thirty pounds. Every woman to whom I have described that sequence of events has told me that I should have asked girls what they liked.

What they were saying is that I should have done research. And that's what I have done for women. I have surveyed several groups of men of various ages and discovered what looks they find attractive.

I got the information for this section in several ways. In some cases I sent out research teams. Using techniques described in earlier chapters, they tested the reactions of various groups of men to women wearing different outfits. Some of this type of research, including the research for the sections on dentists and army officers, was done at hotels during conventions.

I also derived much of the information as a by-product of corporate research into what clothes were effective in a business setting.

Obviously, this information will not guarantee that any woman will be able to attract the man or men she wants to attract. But it should help.

MEN WITH OLD MONEY

The term "old money" stirs images of mansions at Newport, gigantic yachts, galaxies of servants, and fellows who are called "the Third." It is associated with names like Vanderbilt and Rockefeller, people whose dollars, laid end on end, would stretch from Palm Beach to anywhere.

No doubt about it, that's old money. But there aren't very many of those blue bloods. And they don't spend much time in public places, so they're almost unreachable. If you don't meet some of them in school, your chances of meeting them at all are pretty slim. Besides, they usually marry members of their own social set.

I have not researched these people, but statistics on them probably wouldn't be very revealing anyway because they don't have to follow most of the rules that bind the rest of us.

Some of these men, like the Rockefellers, work all their lives. Others lie on Mediterranean beaches (you might meet one there) and amount to wealthy people on welfare. Since these men are the pinnacle of the establishment, they probably have little respect for the demands of the establishment.

Some take the game more seriously than others. I would bet that many a blue blood died with his tie on. Some wouldn't be caught alive or dead in a tie. Others, like Nelson Rockefeller, play the game only as long as they have to. For years Rockefeller was the model politician. He said, "Hiya, Fella." But after he became a lame duck vice-president, he gave hecklers the finger, saying, "Same to ya, Fella."

These men have mothers who were thin and rich, and the women they're attracted to are thin and rich. Their women are buyers of fashion simply because they have the money to go to Paris and pay several thousand dollars for a dress.

The members of this group I have met and worked with tend to be sensible and down to earth. My guess (and I will always tell you when I'm guessing) is that they're not really impressed by a designer label or any other trapping. They simply like what they like, and money is no object.

There are, however, men with old money who are more accessible. They are people with definable limits to their wealth. They might go first class to Cancun twice a year, but they generally don't fly in their own jets. Just the same, they are rich. And their money has been around for a while. This group provides most of the eligible bachelors who could be legitimately described as having real money.

The source of most old money is the family business. The heirs to these businesses tend to go into management of the business, and therefore they become businessmen. As such, they become very conservative in their attitudes and their dress. These men don't *have* to conform, but they wear suits and ties to the office because they think it's the thing to do.

These men like four distinct looks in women: a look of competence; a look of femininity; an athletic, outdoorsy look; and a slightly exotic look.

However, any one of these looks in the wrong setting will irk these men. A woman who looks outdoorsy in a business situation will not click. A woman who looks frilly and feminine for sports will not score points.

The Competent Look

Men who have always been successful (because they inherited success) are not intimidated by authoritative women. In fact, they are attracted to competent women.

If such a man is your boss or if you deal with him in any other business situation, a skirted suit in blue or beige, along with a contrasting blouse, can be an effective seduction garment.

Of course, the look of competence changes from profession to profession. While old-money types will be attracted to someone who looks competent in an office, they will be equally attracted to someone who looks like a competent artist, perhaps in a paint-stained smock.

There is one definite taboo: These men will be totally turned off by any woman who wears masculine clothes. We showed them a picture of a woman in a man-tailored pinstriped suit with a vest, and almost all of them reacted negatively. Most men find this outfit very sexy, but this group objected to it. One man said she looked bitchy or butchy or both.

The Feminine Look

These men are extremely attracted to soft, highly feminine garments. Soft silk dresses ring their bell. Feminine lines, frilly skirts, and lace are all tremendous turn-ons.

The Athletic Look

The younger men in particular like the clean-cut, scrubbed, athletic-girl look. Women who look as if they are outdoors all day interest them. *But* they expect you to look "right" for any activity. If one of these men invites you to play tennis, wear a tennis dress. Make-do outfits, such as cutoff jeans, will bomb.

Your best chance of meeting one of these men is at a resort. That's not particularly hard to do because they take more vacations than most people. The only trick is to go to the right resorts. Cost is one criterion—rich men go to expensive resorts. But it helps to know which ones are "in." If your local paper still has a society section, that might give you clues. You can also check the national gossip columns.

The first rule of resort wear is that you must look as if you know resorts. If, for example, you don't dress casually at Acapulco, you'll look like a first-timer. At some Caribbean resorts, however, the look of the regulars is quite formal. A good travel agent can advise you. If you can't find one you can trust, call your hotel and ask the social director (if there is one) to clue you in. You can then arrive with the right clothes and the right state of mind.

Men with old money like the traditional look in almost everything except resortwear. They like things put out by designers who, like Carol Horn, openly ignore the conservative look. And they are interested in women who, at least in resort wear, seem not to be thinking about their clothes. So don't look as if you are painstakingly put together. Women who go to resorts and then spend Friday night putting their hair up in rollers will turn off the men they probably want most to attract. These men are much more relaxed with women who themselves are relaxed about their appearance.

Their reaction to sportswear is the exact opposite of their reaction to resort wear. In sportswear, the more traditional the better. Your tennis outfit should be a white dress. Your ski wear or riding gear should be in the same traditional mold.

Not only are they interested in women who look out-doorsy, but they also want them to *be* outdoorsy. They are attracted to women who actually do ski, ride, swim, and shoot. So if you go to a ski resort, get out on the slopes. And don't dress as if you are always après-skiing. These men are turned off by women who look as if they just hang around the lounge.

The Slightly Exotic Look

A touch of the exotic fascinates these men. It has to be "Brahman exotic"—the sort of weird, kicky thing that's available only in stores for very rich people. In our testing, these men reacted positively to a necklace of gold golf balls. They are intrigued by such things as sandals with real gold straps, or luggage that is made only in Afghanistan.

We asked these men what caught their eye and got such answers as this one: "Hey, last week I saw a girl in a dress embroidered with shells. I liked it."

You don't want to be dripping with these gee-whiz items. One will be interesting; two will be outrageous.

When any of these items becomes popular, it loses its value as Brahman exotic.

Color and Material

The color preferences of men with old money are amaz-ingly predictable. Apparently their money, not the source of it, is the common thread. Men whose millions came from agriculture react exactly the same as men whose fortunes came from law or manufacturing. They all were attracted to women who wore colors that said upper middle class.

The classic upper middle class combination of blue and beige was their favorite. Their second favorite combination was beige and gray, and their third choice was blue and gray.

They are attracted to women in pure fibers. They recognize and appreciate pure cotton, rich wool, and high-quality silk. They showed a strong preference for dry-clean-only garments. The polyester pantsuit look horrified them.

Women who are involved in social activities and social services interest these men. And, teachers note: We ran a long list of women's occupations past them. The list included lawyer, doctor, accountant, and several other highly prestigious professions. But the one they chose most was schoolteacher.

These men have a unique characteristic: They will usually tell women the truth. We found when we had women ask men in other groups what they thought of their outfit, the men either ducked the question or told a pleasant lie. But these men don't do that. If a woman asks what they like and don't like, they tell her. So if you're dating a man who has old money and you want to know what to wear, ask him. He is probably the only type of man in America who will tell you.

MEN WITH NEW MONEY

There are two kinds of new-money men, the gamblers and those in semisafe businesses.

Both are men who have gone into business for themselves or who have inherited a small business and built it up.

The gambler, or high-risk taker, deals in a highly competitive field and stands to gain or lose barrels of money. This category includes men in construction, advertising, entertainment, and the garment industry. It includes almost all developers and promoters.

Often their business depends on their contacts and their

ability to move socially. Research indicates that they are attracted to women who will help them do that. The women they date and marry have considerable party wardrobes.

They also are attracted to women who dress in a relatively conservative style. They are totally turned off by a woman who wears too much perfume or makeup or who is overtly sexy.

The classic example of the new-money man is The Great Gatsby. He came off the North Dakota prairies, made a lot of money in some shady high-risk ventures, and started throwing lavish parties on Long Island. He was constantly surrounded by actresses, other glitter girls, and fashionable flappers, but he wanted Daisy, the essence of upper middle class.

These men are fascinated by women who know how to handle people. Social clods need not apply.

There is no such thing as a business that is completely safe. But some are relatively low risk. Farming is one of them. Farmers are always in debt, but most of them survive and some of them get rich.

There are plenty of men with semisafe businesses—men who produce such things as machine tools, ball bearings, or other industrial materials and who very quietly and very conservatively pile up mountains of money.

The women they are attracted to reflect their own business styles. They like women in subdued colors: blue, dark brown, and beige. No fashion models for them.

DOCTORS, SCIENTISTS, ACCOUNTANTS, ENGINEERS

Doctors seem to be the favorite target of women who are seeking successful men. They are also the easiest target because they read like a thermometer.

Doctors are attracted to women wearing chic, with-it, up-to-date, and expensive clothing. They prefer thin women whose clothing says they are models and whose actions say they are socialites. They are attracted to women who display obvious status symbols—women who wear labels on their handbags, umbrellas, and anything else a label can be slapped on. If designers start tattooing women, doctors will be the first to applaud. I'm convinced that Mrs. Hippocrates wore designer tunics.

Doctors are notoriously poor dressers who want their women to dress exquisitely. That's why doctors' wives always look as if an expensive closet just fell on them. Doctors are the only group of men in America who will choose an average-looking woman festooned with status symbols over a beautiful woman without them.

To dress for doctors, simply buy whatever is being shown in the *New York Times* or in fashion magazines and wear it even where it isn't appropriate. Doctors have no sense of where clothes are appropriate. They are more attracted to a woman in an expensive dress at a casual picnic in the woods than they are to someone wearing something quite appropriate, like jeans.

Scientists, engineers, and accountants have exactly the opposite reaction. These men have been trained into a sense of completion. They expect all the parts of any apparatus to work in harmony. So they are turned off by anyone who wears the wrong clothes for the occasion or who presents an incomplete or incongruous picture.

Not so with doctors. They're in a guessing game all the time. They never have the whole picture of what's going on in a human body. So they're used to fragmented information, and they don't expect a woman to have a sense of completeness or even congruity in her clothing. And they turn to

155

another criterion, the look of money or status, no matter how badly the look is assembled.

If you're playing touch football, you are far more likely to attract an accountant with a pair of jeans and a dirty sweat shirt than if you are wearing something neater and inappropriate. This is also true about mixing styles. With a doctor you can wear a pair of jeans and a clean, expensive, frilly blouse. An engineer would consider that combination tasteless.

With many engineers and scientists there is another consideration—lines. Their sense of completion extends to line, and they will object to any clash in line. If you wear a scarf with lines that go one way and a dress with lines going another, they will somehow think you're tasteless, and they won't quite know why. All our testing shows that they will be attracted to women who wear all solids, since solids never seem to clash. And they will think that a woman in solids is a better dresser than a woman who wear patterns because patterns, in their mind, never quite work neatly.

Engineers and accountants are attracted to certain colors. They particularly go for blue, pale yellow, beige, and lavender. It's surprising that they like women to wear lavender. Lavender tests as a negative with just about every other group in America. And engineers and accountants don't like or trust other men who wear it. But somehow they find it extremely attractive on a woman. I don't know why.

Scientists and engineers are turned off by any hint of high fashion. They consider fashionable women to be phonies and they will avoid them. They are interested in a woman whose appearance says to them, "I'm down to earth, I'm realistic, and one and one always means two to me."

Therefore, they are equally turned off by obscure styles, strange designs, and unusual colors. Scientists and engineers want to marry Alice Blue Gown—if the gown is solid blue and nothing distracting is worn with it.

CORPORATE BUSINESSMEN

One old saying holds that "when a woman marries a man, she marries his family." In our business-oriented society, when a woman marries a man, she marries his company.

Even though it may seem old-fashioned, when you date a man who is a corporate animal, you are also being courted by his company. In addition to introducing you to his mother, he will also probably introduce you to Mother Corporation.

To impress that latter fussy mother, you must wrap yourself in upper middle class clothing. Anything overtly sexy is disastrous.

You must remember that your man has been trained to conform. Any unusual or exotic item that Mother Corp. might disapprove of can scare him.

At the same time he is constantly seeking success, and therefore any clothing that implies wealth is a strong positive.

Fashion is one of the most important elements. The ideal look for this man is moderately fashionable.

To be moderately fashionable you must

• Never look dated.

• Obey the six-month rule. Never be the first one in your area to wear anything. Wait until it has been around half a year.

• Obey the six-year rule. If any item has been a high-fashion choice for six years, it is automatically acceptable. An example of this would be the A-line dress, which has been worn off and on by fashionable women for fifty years.

• Remember that particular localities dictate the degree to

157

which fashion is acceptable. Let us assume that a new fashion catches on in Paris in the spring and that this fashion eventually will catch on throughout the United States. It will probably not begin to make its impact on New York for at least six months, and possibly a year. It will not make an impact on Des Moines, Omaha, or any other heart-of-America city until a year or two later, which is at least a year and a half after it came out in Paris.

Jumping into a fashion too fast can really hurt. This applies to business situations as well as to the woman who is dating a corporation man. After platform shoes were in New York for six months, a New York businesswoman wore a pair into an office in Des Moines. Her boss in New York got a call later that day asking why they had sent a kook.

• Never assume that the presence of a high-fashion label on a garment makes it acceptable for business.

• Never wear a fashion item that is connected with being antiestablishment. These corporation people *are* the establishment.

PROFESSIONAL ARMY OFFICERS

We did a survey of several hundred professional military men (mostly in the army) and found that they were attracted basically to one type of woman—conservative and well put together. They were appalled by a woman who was in any way sloppy or who wore clothes that seemed too sexy.

We found army officers to be quite sophisticated, probably because so many of them travel the world regularly. They are aware of the international look, which is far more fashionable than the look of the average American woman. Women in most European countries buy a half dozen good outfits and wear them over and over, while American women tend to buy tons of junk. The army officers tend to be attracted to women with a conservative, traditional, almost European look. The best way to describe the look is Bergdorf Goodman chic.

SALESMEN

Salesmen sell. But they like women who buy. So if you want to attract a successful salesman, buy, buy, buy. And be sure you buy the best. Salesmen are drawn to a look of affluence. You probably won't be able to fool them with cheap imitations; they know quality and value.

Successful salesmen are often broke because they and their wives or girl friends throw money around. But don't worry. A good salesman will always make a lot of money—and he'll appreciate a woman who knows how to spend it.

BLUE-COLLAR WORKERS

Blue-collar workers are *not* attracted by lower middle class clothing, our research shows. They themselves may be comfortable in lower middle class clothes, but successful blue-collar workers prefer women who have a sense of style.

Blue-collar workers indicated to us that they think that they earn as much as many professionals and believe that socially they deserve the same degree of respect. They also realize that often they do not get it. That's probably why they are attracted to women who seem to them to have a certain air of style about them.

Their definition of a good dresser is more color-oriented than class-oriented. They will be attracted to a woman who wears moderate amounts of perfume and makeup, whose hair is in place, and who wears well-coordinated clothing. They tend to be attracted to women who are monochromatic. A doctor, a lawyer, or an engineer will find a woman in a tan skirt with a tan blouse and a tan coat rather dull, but blue-collar workers will be definitely attracted to her.

They are turned off by women who look as if they are half prepared for the supermarket and half prepared for something else, such as church or a party.

But most important, they are attracted to women who on dates dress in a way that forces them to wear suits and ties.

And, even though they complain about it after they get married, these men, more than doctors, lawyers, schoolteachers, executives, and salesmen, enjoy taking their women to dress-up places.

In many restaurants where casual attire is the norm, waiters and waitresses assume that men who wear suits or sports coats and ties are plumbers on the town. Men who wear suits and ties all day shed them to go to places like that. They enjoy dressing down and the blue-collar workers enjoy dressing up.

Therefore, if you want to attract or marry a blue-collar worker, a substantial Saturday night wardrobe would be a good investment.

LAWYERS

"Frankly, Mr. Molloy," the new woman lawyer said, "I'm more interested in marrying a partner than becoming one."

This forthright woman had just been hired by a law firm that had engaged me to advise its five new women lawyers on effective dress. She said she would follow my suggestions on dressing to further her career, but what she really wanted to know was what clothes would make her attractive to the male lawyers in the firm.

We discovered that lawyers seem to be attracted to women who look like they would make excellent witnesses. And we learned that lawyers who argue before juries know the value of clothing, since they are constantly sizing up the clothing of prospective jurors.

The lawyers we surveyed like women who wear:
- Expensive, traditional clothing.
- Suede, velvet, and other expensive-looking materials.
- Expensive accessories, such as good silk scarves.
- Dresses in beige, medium and dark blue, white, and pale yellow.

They do not like women who wear:
- Anything that says budget or bargain basement.
- Anything exotic. (While a woman wearing anything blue or yellow would be attractive to them, the same woman wearing a blue that was tinted green or a yellow with a touch of gold would turn them off.)
- Large costume jewelry, noticeable makeup, low-cut blouses, sexy skirts, and anything else that flashes sexuality.

We found lawyers' reactions to color and pattern to be limited. They were affected more by the total look, and the look they strongly preferred was quiet and conservative.

DENTISTS

Young dentists seem to be under the influence of novocaine. Almost nothing turned them on.

They seemed to be attracted to women who strike the exact center chord, and, therefore, they were almost impossible to test. They were turned off by fashionable women; they were turned off by unfashionable women. Gaudy women didn't interest them; plain women didn't interest them. So what to do? Well, about the only information I can offer is that dentists marry "the girl next door." Sorry I can't be more specific.

Dentists over thirty-five, however, showed some preferences. They came off like doctors, with an attraction to money and status. At age forty and above, they showed a preference for women who wear beige dresses and carry designer handbags.

PROFESSORS

Professors tend to be attracted to two types of women: those who appear intellectually gifted and those who appear socially gifted. This involves two definite looks.

The first is the "college campus–who cares?–professorial look." It's tweedy, denimy, youthful, and a bit unkempt. Women professors, particularly the younger ones, dress in a rather nonsexual way. They think it's easier to deal with classes that way. As a result women faculty members are somewhat less put together during their teaching hours than they are in their off-hours. But male professors like the dowdy look.

The second look is the exact opposite. The same professor who finds a woman colleague attractive in dowdy clothing will also be attracted to the fashion-model type. He will not be attracted to a woman who falls somewhere in between.

Professors like women to wear earth colors—beige, brown, and rust. More consistently than any other group, they picked women in these colors or combinations of these colors as being most attractive, most desirable, most appealing, and most compatible.

MEN IN HIGH-RISK PROFESSIONS

Policemen, firemen, and other men with high-risk jobs want low-risk women. They are upset by women who break with expectation. They would be turned off by a woman who showed up at a formal social event in jeans or by a woman who wore a party dress to an informal jeans party.

So far they parallel scientists and engineers. But these high-risk guys carry it one step further. If your clothes say to them that you are a college graduate or a professional woman, they will be turned off if you are not. It's not that they're after status but rather that they are bothered by anyone who seems to be telling a nonverbal lie. They want people to be exactly what they seem.

Their favorite colors on women are blue, very soft beige, rust, and a whole series of nonaggressive pastels—pale pink, pale yellow, pale green. They don't like to see women in dark brown, black, or lavender.

ARTISTS, MUSICIANS, WRITERS

Visual artists—painters, sculptors, and so forth—are attracted to women whose clothes are a clue that they have some artistic ability.

There are two ways a woman can deliver that message. One requires all the artistic skill of dumping a bucket of paint on a canvas; the other requires thought, skill, and a sixth sense of what works.

With the first method, the idea is to look like an artist, since artists are attracted to fellow artists. Women artists usually dress extremely casual, often bordering on sloppiness. Sometimes they completely ignore their appearance. And that haphazard approach seems to go over with male artists.

The second method requires some effort because male artists also react positively to women who show artistic ability by putting their clothes together beautifully—particularly women who use color well. They are not interested in the high-fashion type but rather in women who can put together tricky combinations and make them work. Almost all our male artists chose as attractive a woman wearing a yellow blouse, green skirt, and an orange sleeveless sweater, and carrying a multicolored handbag. Although that combination sounds awful, it actually worked.

They also were attracted to women who wore monochromatic ensembles—four or five variations of one color—and made them work well. This was the only highly educated group that was strongly attracted to a monochromatic look.

Musicians and writers tend to be attracted to women who are somewhat clothes conscious and who dress in a manner that, if not fashionable, is at least quite presentable.

We found musicians' favorite colors to be bright red, orange, yellow, and green. Writers, however, displayed no particular color preference. They were more interested in definition of line and more attracted to a woman whose clothing was cut beautifully rather than one whose clothing was colored beautifully. Writers tended to be attracted to women who wore soft, flowing dresses.

Unfortunately, we could not round up many writers or musicians. The foregoing is based on interviews with twenty-five in each category, which is hardly a substantial number.

MEN IN HIGH-FASHION INDUSTRIES

If I were to guess ahead of time which people would be least likely to take this book seriously, I would pick those who are dedicated to the belief that looking chic, fashionable, and up to date is important. On the other hand, if I were challenged to prove that what you wear evokes a conditioned response from the people you meet, I would use this surprisingly predictable group to prove it.

Men who follow fashion can be found in important positions in several industries: advertising, television, the fashion industry itself, and a handful of other fields.

There is also a sprinkling of such men in the mainstream

of American business. But almost invariably they are going nowhere because fashion fails.

On several occasions we tested men who are high-fashion dressers. One of the most revealing research projects involved the midi. When the midi first came on the scene, we tested men and women across a broad range of American society, and their reaction was highly negative.

This high-fashion group was no exception. The men in this group generally thought the midi was ugly and unbecoming. When we ran twin tests of the same woman wearing the midi and a shorter skirt, they invariably picked the woman in the shorter skirt as being sexier, more appealing, more clever, more intelligent, and so on.

Six months later, however, after the fashion moguls had dictated to their disciples that the midi was a must, their reaction changed, while the rest of the country's reaction stayed about the same. When we went back and asked these men which woman was more clever, more intelligent, sexier, and more appealing, the woman in the midi was the big winner. Ninety-two percent of the men had changed their minds.

If you want to attract a man who is fashionable or who works in a high-fashion environment, you must carefully read *Women's Wear Daily*, *Vogue*, and all the other organs of the fashion world. You must not adopt a fashion the day it comes out. But six months after it hits, it becomes an absolute must.

We are not sure exactly where in that six-month period the change takes place, but the change is so dramatic that I'm sure a woman who is tuned into fashion will pick it up immediately.

That 92 percent surprisingly included men in high-fashion industries who themselves do not dress in a high-fashion manner. Many of the male leaders of high-fashion industries dress in traditional garments. If they wear a sports jacket and slacks, the sports jacket is most likely to be blue and the slacks traditional charcoal gray.

Another important factor is the quality of clothes. Men who are themselves interested in clothing can tell the difference between clothing that is expensive and that which is *very* expensive. They are highly attracted to women who spend a great deal of money on clothing. They will not only recognize but appreciate an all-silk dress, an expensive wool coat, or a quality fur. Most men in other industries, at least on the surface, couldn't care less.

Expensive jewelry is also a strong positive.

The affinity of these men to women with expensive goods is not a form of fortune hunting. In fact, many of these men indicated in interviews that they would not be attracted to a rich woman who dressed poorly.

More than any other group, high-fashion men think of their women as decorations. Many give lip service to the idea of the liberated woman, but what they really want is a woman they can brag about and show off.

Chapter 7

For the Consumer

Any woman anywhere can get more for less. Here are some tips on how to do it.

BUYING IT CHEAP

• Measure the price against use. A pair of jeans you can wear every day that cost $15 is a better buy than a pair of velvet pants that costs $20, even if the jeans are not on sale and the velvet pants regularly cost $100. The fashion industry spends millions of dollars every year telling women that being impractical is feminine. It's not. It's stupid.

• Buy on sale. Classic items in traditional styles and colors that can be worn to work time and time again are the best purchases at the end of a season. It is not a good idea to buy a fad or fashion item at the end of a season.

We conducted a five-year experiment with sixty women. We asked them to record the items they bought at the end of a season, the price, and how much wear they got out of them. We found that when they bought traditional items, 86 percent of the time they were very happy with their purchase two to four years later and thought they had made an excellent buy. When they bought fashion or fad items, they were almost invariably displeased. Those items almost never came out of the closet.

• Make sure that markdowns are legitimate. If you don't know quality, workmanship, or material, keep a little notebook of the prices of the items you like. Be sure to note the exact price, the date, and the brand. If you run across the same item or one very similar to it, you'll be better able to judge what it's really worth. In a survey of 120 markdowns in a cross-section of stores throughout the United States, we found that 66 percent of the stores did exactly what they said they were doing. They were marking the item down. The rest were marked down less than the store said or they were not marked down at all. Not nice.

• If you can, buy merchandise with a label that includes a store's name. Stores will put their name only on garments that they are sure are going to last. After all, if the inside of your coat is tattered after six months and the label says "Pierre d'Something," it's hard to get to Paris to complain. Even if you do get there, Pierre doesn't care. But if your store is down on the corner, you're going to pack up the remains of the garment and shake them at the manager. He knows that. And he does care. Buyers are very cautious in choosing the items on which they put the store brand. Use this information to your advantage.

• A designer item, even when it's on sale, is no bargain. You are always paying something extra for having the designer's name on the garment. Designers don't live on yachts and make a million dollars in a year because they're stupid. They make it because buyers are stupid.

• If you think you need designer clothing, check and see if you can find out which manufacturer makes it in your section of the country. The same manufacturer may make something comparable in quality but without the designer label that adds cost to the garment. Try asking the store who the manufacturer is. Sometimes they'll tell you.

• When you can, buy clothing in boys' and men's shops or in Army Navy Surplus stores. Generally, the quality is higher and the price is lower. For example, jeans and corduroy pants tailored to fit are excellent buys. Boys' shirts can be used by some women as man-tailored shirts. Always buy men's cuff links. They are cheaper; they are better; and they last longer. Sweaters, T-shirts, and thermal underwear are the best items available for the woman who likes outdoor living. This fact was discovered by college kids, who have limited funds, and they are right, right, right.

• The cost of a garment must include the cost of the upkeep. A label that says "Dry Clean Only" usually adds 100 percent to the cost of the garment. It adds a higher percentage to the cost of a cheap garment.

• Whenever possible, buy in downtown stores. That's where you'll stand your chance of getting higher quality and lower prices.

• Whenever you can, buy at discount outlets. The most common types are the following:

1. *Factory outlets.* They're legitimate when they're next

to a factory and may be legitimate even when they're not. (But if you don't see any factory and you don't know what you're doing, forget that place.) You should expect at least a 40 percent discount from these outlets, and you can get as much as 50 percent off.

Most of the merchandise will be first quality, but much of it will be irregulars. Retailers ship irregular merchandise back to the factory, and the factory outlet is just a way of getting rid of it. You should never buy an item that you have not examined carefully.

2. *Wholesalers' outlets.* These are really factory outlets for several factories. Your main worry in this type of outlet is not irregulars, since wholesalers' outlets will ship irregulars back to the factory. What you will have to watch out for is the artificial markup. When a factory owns the outlet, it simply can produce more items to keep its factory store open. However, a wholesaler's outlet depends strictly on the overruns and mistakes made by the factory. If the factory doesn't happen to have overruns at the moment, the wholesaler, in order to keep his place operating, will buy cheap merchandise and sell it at a profit rather than sell expensive merchandise at a markdown. For example, if the wholesaler is selling $12 shirts for $6, he may also sell $6 shirts, which look like $12 shirts, for $6. No discount for you.

Watch out for tricky designer names you haven't heard of. If you're going to buy at a wholesaler's outlet—and I suggest that you do—visit it often so you get to know its regular line of good merchandise and avoid everything else.

3. *Manufacturers' outlets.* These are basically the same as factory outlets, but they usually act for several factories. The markdowns in these places are generally

one-third, and they come closer to being retail stores without a middleman.

4. *Stores that buy overruns.* If you're near a large metropolitan area, such as New York, Chicago, or Los Angeles, you will find that there are stores that buy up overruns. They're usually right in the middle of town, and you can make very good purchases there.

• Never buy seconds unless you know exactly what is wrong with the item and you can live with it. If you're going to gamble, gamble on the irregulars, which usually are less seriously damaged than the seconds.

• Figure in the price of alteration before you decide to buy. Women's garments are not altered free. If a woman buys a pair of slacks for $40, she still has to pay extra for any alteration. If a man buys it for $20, that $20 includes the alterations. How do you like that bit of sexism?

HOW TO CROSS-SHOP

Try cross-shopping if you want to upgrade your wardrobe without spending any more money than you now spend. Cross-shopping is a term and a system I invented. It simply means comparing the merchandise in the most expensive stores to the merchandise in less expensive stores and then buying, in your price range, the items that come closest to those in the most expensive stores. It works.

To cross-shop properly, you have to follow a strict procedure. Your objective usually will be to buy clothes that come across as upper middle class. That can be tricky, particularly if you come from a lower socioeconomic background or are not aware of the subtle socioeconomic differences in clothing. If that is your situation, here are two rules.

• For the first three years, only buy traditional colors and patterns.

• Only buy items that you could describe over the phone to a friend and have her know what you are describing. That will mean that the items are easy to wear.

No matter what your background is, you should buy only conservative items that have been around at least a year and a half. You are never to lead in fashion because people who lead in fashion follow in almost everything else.

If you come from a small town, you may have to make special trips to a big city to gain this specialized skill. But it is well worth it.

Cross-shopping must be carried out in the following way.

1. Determine the function of the garment you need. "I need something to wear to work."

2. List the things that will be suitable for you to wear to work. (The other sections of this book will help you make a realistic list.) The item will probably be a dark-colored suit or dress.

3. Go to the best store that is available to you and look at your three top choices—perhaps a blue suit, a gray suit, and a beige dress. Look carefully at them and look at the accessories that are shown with them. Note specifically the price of the items, the look and feel of the material, the cut, the detailing, the buttons, the length, the style, and, above all, the shade of color. (The shade of blue, the shade of gray, or the shade of beige that is available in the swanky store may not be available at your price, thus eliminating the garment as a suitable choice.)

4. Leave the store and go to the least expensive store in town. Go through the cheap store very carefully and attempt to match the expensive ensembles that you have just studied. It is best if there is no more than a lapse of twenty-five or thirty minutes between stores because color memory fades within a half hour for

many people. Obviously you will not be able to match any of the garments exactly, but you should come close on some.

5. Go back to the best store in town for another look, particularly at those items that you came closest to matching in the cheap store.
6. Go to a store in your price range, decide which items come closest to the ones in the expensive store, and buy accordingly.

After you have done this for several years, you will be able to buy the right clothes with only one trip to the expensive store. And, without spending a fortune, you can look rich and successful.

An example of cross-shopping would be a young lawyer who needs a blue, a gray, or a brown suit. She decides that her first choice is blue, her second choice is gray, and her third choice is brown.

She would go to the best store in town and look at the blue, gray, and brown suits. She would find that all three were made of wool, were very well tailored, and had a soft luxuriant look. She would then go to the least expensive store in town and perhaps find that a blue suit there came very close, that a gray suit that didn't come quite as close looked a bit richer, and that a brown suit looked terrible. So she would immediately eliminate the brown suit.

Then she would go back to the expensive store and look carefully at the blue and the gray.

Then she would go to a medium-priced store and find that it had suits in colors almost exactly duplicating both the blue and the gray, but in less expensive material. Only the gray, however, seemed to maintain its luxuriant look. Therefore her best choice at a moderate price would probably be the gray.

If the women reading this book pay attention to no other section except the few preceding paragraphs on cross-shopping, the book will have been at least worth its price.

I have taught thousands of women to cross-shop. Most of them have enjoyed it and looked upon it as a sport. Others have hated it. But 1,307 of the 1,312 women we surveyed before this book was written said that they learned a great deal from it.

Of these, about 20 percent were daughters of people who had money, power, and prestige. Even they had learned that there were certain subtle elements in clothing that had escaped them because for years they had looked only at expensive clothes. They knew what to look for, but they didn't know what to avoid. Therefore, I would suggest that every woman make cross-shopping a regular practice.

A BATTLE OF THE SEXES

Does a woman's clothing dollar go as far as a man's?

I set up a six-month experiment with several couples around the country. My wife, Maureen, and I took part.

Maureen bought a corduroy pantsuit for $78. She paid another $2.50 for alterations. I bought a similar leisure suit for $67 and my pants were tailored free. (The thirteen women in the experiment paid 26 percent more for their garments, which were the closest match they could find to the men's garments.)

We wore our outfits only on days when we were going to be doing the same things. The only difference was that I did more physical things, like moving office furniture.

Six months and eighteen cleanings later, Maureen refused to wear her pantsuit any more. She had sewn two seams and replaced one button. It had shrunk and grown stiff, and there was puckering at the seams.

Since the experiment was over, I stopped having my suit dry-cleaned and started throwing it in the washer and dryer. At this writing, six months after the experiment ended, my suit is still in excellent shape.

Twelve other couples completed the experiment. Two of them reported that the woman's garment performed as well as the man's. One of the satisfied couples had bought jeans, the other raincoats.

In the remaining ten cases, the women felt they had been taken. In most cases the husbands were more indignant about the inequities than were the wives. It was quite an awakening for them.

COMPLAINTS WOMEN HAVE ABOUT THE FASHION INDUSTRY

Since I have been writing my syndicated newspaper column, I have received mail from many women who are furious at the fashion industry. Here are some of the things that my readers want to know.

1. Why, in the same store, when a man buys a pair of slacks for $20 and a woman buys a pair for $80, does the woman have to pay for tailoring while the man gets it free?
2. Why are some people who sew men's garments paid more than people who sew women's garments?
3. Why do women's blouses often cost twice as much as comparable men's shirts?
4. Why do women's sweaters cost more than comparable men's sweaters?
5. Why do many stores not carry cotton and wool alternatives to polyester?
6. Why aren't there standard sizes in women's clothing?

7. Why can't a woman buy shoes with arches without looking like her grandmother or Mammy Yokum?
8. Why do the seams in women's clothes fall apart three or four times as often as the seams in men's clothing?
9. Why don't manufacturers give extra buttons with all coats and dresses that have unusual buttons?
10. Why do manufacturers continue to use plastic thread that can cause skin irritation?
11. When the fashion industry introduces a new item, why doesn't it give women a real choice instead of limiting their choice by withdrawing all the alternatives from the marketplace?

Chapter 8

The Company Spouse

These guidelines will certainly be helpful to any woman who is about to become an "executive wife." Those who have had years of experience in the role might pick up some tips. Many experienced executive wives who gave excellent advice were themselves making some major mistakes.

These guidelines should also help any woman build her social wardrobe.

ADVICE FOR THE EXECUTIVE WIFE

Some wives of businessmen are annoyed when companies make demands on them. They shouldn't be.

177

When a corporation is interested in the spouse of an employee, that employee is important. So if the company shows an interest in you, it's a compliment to your husband. He either has an important job, is being considered for one, or is being groomed for one somewhere down the line. (Or he's in a job where entertaining is important.)

Executives of major corporations probably would like to say that they don't care who their employees are married to. But, being pragmatic, they often do care. They have statistical evidence showing that an employee's marriage affects job performance. And further, they know that at higher levels it is almost inevitable that there will be times when executives' spouses will, in effect, be representing the company.

A wife probably can't put her husband in the boardroom. But she can keep him out. It's a good idea, therefore, to at least know the rules of the corporate spouse game. Some wives of executives are experts at that game.

For the last three years I have been conducting individual interviews with executive wives, holding group sessions, and examining their wardrobes. In the process I have interviewed 100 wives of executives.

The first two interviews, which were in Missouri, promised to be wildly contrasting.

Subject Number One was married to the president and part owner of a substantial company. She entertained frequently in her $250,000 house and at their club. Her wardrobe would have been the envy of Cleopatra and she had an arsenal of jewelry.

Subject Number Two was married to an engineer who was on the first rung of management. Her wardrobe was simple and she had a few modest jewels.

Both women were in their thirties.

I did not tell the women what day I was going to show up. I wanted to catch them off guard to see what they normally wore for their daily chores.

Number One was wearing a pair of $80 wool slacks, a cashmere sweater, and a gold chain. Number Two wore denim pants and a blouse.

But that's as far as the contrasts went. Not only did their answers parallel each other's, but they proved to be highly representative of the answers given in the subsequent 98 interviews. This, of course, indicates that there is a standard look for the executive wife.

The purpose of the first question was not only to get information but also to make the interview fun. We told each woman this: "Imagine you had a friend who ran off to live on a desert when she was fifteen. For fifteen years she wore nothing but jeans and T-shirts. One day at age thirty, she shows up at your doorstep, wearing jeans, a T-shirt, and sandals—the only clothes she owns. She tells you she just got married to an executive who makes $35,000 a year and that her husband gave her several thousand dollars to assemble an adequate wardrobe. She has come to you for advice on what to buy. What would you suggest?

Here are the wardrobes they suggested:

Pants Outfits

NUMBER ONE (the president's wife): Blue, beige, and black wool slacks, accompanied by blue, beige, and gray sweaters. A white blouse, a pale blue blouse, and a patterned blouse with strong contrast that contained the colors of at least two of the pairs of slacks.

NUMBER TWO (the engineer's wife): Two pairs of wool slacks and contrasting sweaters (she didn't specify color). A pair of jeans with appropriate tops to wear around the house.

Skirts

NUMBER ONE: Two or three skirts, one tweed (no colors specified).

NUMBER TWO: "At least one good skirt" with one or two appropriate tops. She specifically mentioned a good silk blouse.

Everyday Dresses

NUMBER ONE: Two or three "classic" dresses. Blue, black, and beige.

NUMBER TWO: Three or four "simple" dresses. Blue, beige, and maroon.

I prodded them to define "classic" and "simple." Both definitions described dresses that don't identify the year they were made, are solid in color, and have no frills.

Semiformal Wear

NUMBER ONE: Three skirts—one wool, one matte jersey (one of these should be white or black), and a summer skirt made of a soft material. (She didn't recommend specific tops.)

NUMBER TWO: One long winter skirt and one long summer skirt with several "nice" tops.

They both said the skirts would be used at some formal gathering and at cocktail parties at three o'clock in the afternoon or later, when they were apt to drift outdoors in nice weather.

Blazer and Suit

NUMBER ONE: One good blazer plus one tweed suit.

NUMBER TWO: A simple blue suit with a blazer. (The blazer, she said, could be worn with other outfits.)

Formal Dresses

Both women agreed that their friend would need one or two formal dresses with jackets.

In this category, as in most categories, Number One was suggesting higher-priced items.

Both said she should avoid fad items, particularly in this category.

Accessories

For formal occasions, both mentioned a black silk and a gold mesh purse.

Number One specified expensive T-strap shoes. Number Two said "nice" T-strap shoes would do.

Number One recommended five or six "good pairs of shoes" plus a designer bag and a dozen designer scarves. She specified that the shoes would have to go with specific garments.

Number Two recommended three pairs of shoes (two pairs of pumps and one pair of walking shoes).

GENERAL GUIDELINES

The general wardrobe advice the 100 women gave to the hypothetical thirty-year-old woman fresh from the desert can be summed up very simply:

• The women agreed that the executive's wife should have three or four simple dresses that are classic in design and in solid colors. The most popular colors suggested were blue, beige, maroon, black, pale yellow, pale green, and deep green.

• The women felt that she should have several pairs of slacks and several skirts. Most recommended good wool tailored slacks and skirts —both slacks and skirts coordinated with several blouses and several sweaters.

• Most of the women recommended some sort of party-going attire. For entertaining at home, they mentioned party pajamas, caftans, hostess gowns, and other similar items. Most of the women whose husbands earned less than $40,000 a year said they generally did not wear these clothes when they entertained. They saved semi-formal wear for large parties.

• All of the women agreed that an executive's wife needs long formal dresses, usually with accompanying jackets. (The richer women suggested more such dresses than women in lower income brackets.) Most agreed that solid-colored dresses were best for women with a limited wardrobe.

• Most agreed that an executive's wife should have a few good pieces of jewelry.

• There was general agreement that the executive's wife had to wear the status symbols of her particular group, which could include everything from designer bags to mink coats.

• Most felt that some skills were necessary. Bridge, tennis, and golf were mentioned frequently. Other activities ranged from bird-watching to rowing. Most stressed that it was important to join in activities with other corporate wives.

Most of these women warned against overdressing. Yet in that area, they led the parade.

OVERDRESSERS ANONYMOUS

Without telling them why, I asked the women to dress in their six favorite party outfits, and I had them photographed. (Fifty-seven of the 100 agreed to participate in this project.) I showed each woman the pictures of the other women. (I switched cities and companies so that the women didn't know each other.)

The women judged their peers to be overdressed 28 percent of the time.

I did further testing and found out that:

1. The older women whose husbands were in more powerful positions were more likely to overdress than the younger women.
2. The less education a woman had the more likely she was to overdress.
3. If a woman came from a lower-class background, she was three times more likely to overdress than if she came from a solid upper middle class background.
4. The women who overdressed judged other women who dressed as they themselves did to be overdressed. Their reaction was surprisingly similar to alcoholics who do not admit that they are alcoholics.

Test to see if you should join *Overdressers Anonymous*. If four or more of the following apply to you, you are an overdresser.

1. You wear jewelry in the afternoon that can be worn in the evening.
2. Over half of your shoes have open toes even when they're not in style.
3. You hardly ever wear low-heeled shoes.
4. Your glasses have rhinestones or other decorations.
5. Over one-third of the clothes in your closet are or were fad items.
6. You spend 50 percent more for your clothes than most women in your social circle.
7. You think you must run out and buy the latest items in order to keep up.

8. You wear false eyelashes in the daytime.
9. You come from a lower socioeconomic background than most of your social circle.

If you think you have to join *Overdressers Anonymous*, don't worry. You don't have to go to any meetings. You can form a one-woman club and hold meetings before a mirror. You can quit *Overdressers Anonymous* if you can stand up at twenty consecutive meetings and say

1. "The garments I am wearing are tailored, traditional, and conservative in color."
2. "My makeup is understated and will appear conservative compared to the makeup of other women."
3. "I am not wearing jewelry or makeup that normally would be associated with nighttime wear."
4. "I am not following any fad."
5. "I am dressed appropriately for the activity I'm going to participate in."

Dress for Success Guidelines

The right clothes can help a woman enormously in achieving success in her business and social life.

This book is a reference work that you'll turn to many times for details on the right look for you in a particular situation. If you keep the following principles in mind, you'll never go too far wrong.

NEVER

- be the first in your office to wear a fashion. Fashion fails.
- wear anything sexy to the office. If you wear something sexy, it is not your brain you are selling.

- wear the knit polyester pantsuit.
- wear pants when you're dealing with men in business.
- dress like an "imitation man."
- carry a handbag when you could carry an attaché case.
- wear a midi unless it's a raincoat or a coat worn over a long dress.
- buy a fad item.
- let the fashion industry dictate skirt length in your businesswear.
- take off your jacket in the office.
- wear designer glasses.
- have more than one drink at a business meeting.
- wear a vest for business.
- make an emotional decision about a piece of clothing when an intellectual decision is possible.

ALWAYS

- wear the skirted suit only for business.
- tailor your clothing to the demands of your job and your company.
- wear upper middle class clothing.
- wear plain pumps to the office.
- wear neutral-colored pantyhose to the office.
- wear a coat that covers your skirt or dress.
- carry an executive gold pen.
- have a neuter rather than a masculine or feminine office.
- buy your sportswear at high-quality stores.
- ask yourself who you are going to meet and what you are going to do before you get dressed.
- check this book before you go shopping.

How To Get Your Personal Dress for Success Profile

Now that this book has demonstrated the principles of successful business/professional/social/leisure wear for you, here's how to apply these concepts directly to your own personality, body type, and career goals.

The author of THE WOMAN'S DRESS FOR SUCCESS BOOK, John T. Molloy, has systematized the results of his eighteen-year wardrobe research in a computerized information bank. His advice will be geared to a changing environment and your own characteristics including your:

Height	Skin Coloring	Your Business/Profession
Weight	Hair Color	Present Occupation
Age	Personality Type	Company Affiliation
		Education and Career Target

When you send in the coupon (page 189), America's first wardrobe engineer will send you a questionnaire. He will then match your information against the combined results of his total research and apply it to scientifically tailor your personal successful wardrobe for you.

The program is for businesswomen and wives of businessmen.

Find out: What colors are best for you/What styles are best for you/How to make the most of your physical characteristics/How to dress to get a raise, a promotion, an order from a top client/...And much, much more.

Take the first step toward the most successful appearance that modern research can tailor for you and fill in this coupon today.

HOW TO GET YOUR PERSONAL DRESS
FOR SUCCESS PROFILE

John T. Molloy, America's first wardrobe engineer, has been constructing personal profiles based on research for the leaders of government and industry for the past twenty-two years. He is now one of America's most sought after and highest paid corporate image consultants. He has taken his research and, with the help of a computer, he now makes it available to you.

The personal profile will give you advice based on your height, weight, coloring, position, company affiliation, geography, career goals, personal preferences, and other variables too numerous to mention. In addition, the program prints out a list of thirty-five suits, shirts, and ties in the order of their researched preference for your success. There are millions of possibilities in this section of the program alone. The advice is very specific and geared to you.

The advice is also geared to the changing environment we live in and is constantly updated. A new and expanded program is now available for $24.95 for either men or women.

Mr. John T. Molloy
P.O. Box 526
Wash-bridge Station
New York, NY 10033

Dear Mr. Molloy:

Please send me your new personalized DRESS FOR SUCCESS Questionnaire. I understand that 6 weeks after I return my filled-in questionnaire to you, I will receive my complete wardrobe profile.

_____ Enclosed is a check for $24.95 to cover the cost of the profile.

_____

Last Name (Please print)　　　First Name　　　Middle Initial

_____

Address　　　　City　　　　State　　　　Zip

Help Yourself and Your Career

___HOW TO MAKE A HABIT OF SUCCESS
by Bernard Haldane   (K30-501, $3.50)

The Haldane system is one of the most important success and self-improvement books recently published. Its self-identification process and Success Factor Analysis techniques have become integral to career planning programs in leading institutions such as Harvard and Columbia Universities and The Peace Corps. Change your career by using your personal interests and talents in a new way.

___POSITIONING: THE BATTLE FOR YOUR MIND
by Al Ries and Jack Trout   (K30-800, $3.95)

"Positioning" is the first body of thought to come to grips with the problems of communicating in an overcommunicated (too many companies, too many products, too many media, too much marketing noise) society.

You will learn in detail some unique concepts that can help you master the media: climbing the product ladder; *cherchez le creneau* (look for the hole); repositioning the competition; avoiding the no-name trap; and avoiding the line-extension trap.

___GETTING ORGANIZED   *large format paperback*
by Stephanie Winston   *(J37-956, $6.95, U.S.A.)*
                                                 (J37-957, $8.50, Canada)

Guidelines to organization covering everything from financial to meal planning, maximization of storage space, living space and reduction of time required to complete everyday tasks.

___DRESS FOR SUCCESS   *large format paperback*
by John T. Molloy   *(K37-381, $6.95, U.S.A.)*
                                                 (K37-382, $7.95, Canada)

The number-one book to make you look like a million so you can *make* a million will: make it easier for many men to sell everything better: open doors to the executive suite to men for whom they are now closed; make the right wardrobe less expensive; give women a simple, sensible guide to buying men's clothing; and teach men how women like them to dress.

WARNER BOOKS
P.O. Box 690
New York, N.Y. 10019

Please send me the books I have checked. I enclose a check or money order (not cash), plus 50¢ per order and 50¢ per copy to cover postage and handling.* (Allow 4 weeks for delivery.)

_____ Please send me your free mail order catalog. (If ordering only the catalog, include a large self-addressed, stamped envelope.)

Name _____

Address _____

City _____

State _____ Zip _____

*N.Y. State and California residents add applicable sales tax.   72

IMPROVE YOUR CAREER
WITH WARNER BOOKS